# SILICONNED

# SILICONNED

How the tech industry solves fake problems, hoards idle workers, and makes doomed bets with other people's money

Emmanuel Maggiori, PhD

Copyright © 2024 Emmanuel Maggiori
All rights reserved. No part of this book may be reproduced in any manner without written permission except in the case of brief quotations embodied in critical articles and reviews.
Published by Applied Maths Ltd
Paperback ISBN: 978-1-8383372-5-4
E-book ISBN: 978-1-8383372-6-1
Hardcover ISBN: 978-1-8383372-7-8

# CONTENTS

| | | |
|---|---|---|
| Introduction | | 7 |
| 1. | Miracles | 13 |
| 2. | Explosive Growth | 43 |
| 3. | Venture Capital | 67 |
| 4. | Cheap Money, Free Money | 99 |
| 5. | Recipes for Unproductivity | 131 |
| 6. | What We Can Do | 161 |
| Final Thoughts | | 183 |
| Acknowledgments | | 187 |
| Notes | | 189 |
| Index | | 219 |

# INTRODUCTION

An enthusiastic Twitter employee posted a video called, "Day in my life at the Twitter office!"[1] As we see images of the facilities, the employee explains, "I started my morning off with an iced matcha from the café. Then I had a meeting, so I quickly scheduled one of these little pod rooms which are so cool—they're literally noise-canceling. I took my meeting and got ready for brunch. Look how delicious this food looks. Oh, my goodness! I was so overwhelmed!"

After we see the food, the video goes on. "Then, I made my way down to this log cabin area. I don't know what this is, but it is really cool. I played some foosball with my friends to kind of unwind a bit. Also, I found this really cool meditation room that I thought was super neat. I don't do any yoga, but they have this yoga room if you're a yogi, so also that is really cool. I had a couple more meetings in the afternoon—I had a ton of projects that we needed to knock out. I then went to the library to kind of get some more work done. Obviously, we had to have our afternoon coffee, so I made some espresso and then, before leaving for the day, I had some red wine—that's on tap—and went out to the rooftop and just honestly enjoyed the beautiful weather."

A few months later, Twitter fired 75% of its employees.

A *Washington Post* reporter predicted that Twitter's layoffs would be detrimental to the company. The article suggested, "Layoffs of that magnitude mean critical operations running at half strength. It means accidentally firing the only person who knew how to perform some core business function."[2]

But Twitter kept running pretty smoothly. Three months later, the *Washington Post* reporter acknowledged that, despite a couple of "transient service issues" and political objections to the company's direction, Twitter was doing fine. The article asked, "If Twitter can get by for three months on a fraction of its staff, how many of those folks were actually necessary?"[3] Twitter (later renamed X) continued its layoffs—within a couple of years, it had reduced its headcount by 90% from its peak.

The Twitter layoffs were not an isolated incident; they were part of a dramatic downfall of the tech industry, which started in 2022. During this downfall, massive layoffs plagued the entire industry, affecting both start-ups and giants like Google and Amazon. In addition, the amount of investment in tech collapsed and start-ups failed at record rates.

The crash happened after the tech sector had gone a little crazy—in the years preceding the crash, the sector had received more money than ever and could afford splurging it on all sorts of things, such as hiring too many people and equipping offices with lavish supplies.

During those crazy years, tech companies could also afford to do the most outlandish experiments. For example, a start-up called Quibi spent over a billion dollars of investors' money to create short videos featuring A-list Hollywood stars. These videos were meant to populate its video streaming platform, which hadn't even been launched yet. The company never validated whether people actually wanted to see that type of content. When the platform launched, reception of the content wasn't great, and the start-up collapsed just six months later.

Another crazy start-up was Juicero, which built a Wi-Fi-connected juice-pressing machine that sold for $699. The machine took capsules filled with fruit, which cost $5 each, and pressed them to produce glasses of juice. The start-up received a whopping $120 million from investors to build and commercialize the machine. The company went bust because, quite predictably, very few people bought it. In addition, those who bought it were soon disappointed when they realized they could just press the fruit capsules with their hands and squeeze out equally fine juice.

During those crazy years, it seemed as if the tech sector was running on an unlimited wallet. It also seemed like the bar of due diligence had dropped quite low. The start-up WeWork, for example, received billions from investors despite having a business model that didn't quite add up. The founder made hundreds of millions by selling his shares privately behind the scenes, right before the company started to break beyond repair. A more bitter example was that of FTX, a fraudulent cryptocurrency start-up which received nearly two billion dollars from investors. Its founder is now in jail.

This wasn't the first time tech had gone crazy; it had already happened a decade before in what became known as the dot-com bubble. If nothing changes, it may continue to happen over and over again.

Even if you have little to do with tech, you have good reasons to be concerned about all this, as tech's tendency to go crazy impacts us all. For example, as we'll discuss later, money from the general public—such as pension pots, university tuitions, and taxes—is often used to fund tech's activities. It's *your* money.

## WHY WE'RE HERE

I am a software engineer specialized in artificial intelligence. Since I was a little kid, I've been fascinated by computers and all sorts of machines. When I grew up, I wanted to build useful things—that's why I chose this career path. My experience working in tech, however, was extremely unfulfilling. Much like the Twitter employee from that video, I often found myself with little work to do or none at all.

For example, a company once hired me to join a technology team that was building cutting-edge software to assist artificial intelligence engineers. On my first day, it turned out they'd hired dozens of us without really knowing what we would work on. So, they put me "on the bench" until they could find me something to do. I was officially paid to do nothing. This wasn't as fun as it may sound because it required a lot of waiting around by a computer and even doing make-believe work.

In other cases, I did manage to find work to do. However, my job was often to help build an outlandish product that had little chances of ever being used. Other times, it was to hype up a product, for example, by telling clients that artificial intelligence worked better than it really did. I had the impression that finding useful work to do in tech was quite difficult.

This made me worried about the future of the tech sector, so I decided to share my experience with others. I wrote an article about all this and published it on my blog. Its title was, "I've been employed in tech for years, but I've almost never worked." The article went viral, and hundreds of techies reached out to me to share their stories. A lot of them told me they were idle at work and depressed about it, as it was not what they had in mind when they chose this career path. Since then, many stories of idle tech employees have made headlines around the world.

I started doing research to understand why the tech sector had this tendency to go crazy—there must be identifiable reasons for it. In order to find out, I spoke with many techies, entrepreneurs, venture capitalists, and economists. During our conversations, some common themes popped up, such as low interest rates, misaligned incentives, productivity-killing work practices, and even infamous investment scams like Ponzi schemes. After many conversations, I decided to organize my thoughts and put them together in a book. So, here we are.

This book shares my findings with you. I hope it will be informational but also a bit funny and outrageous sometimes—the extravagance of tech can go so far that it can make you laugh and shake your head.

## HOW THIS BOOK IS ORGANIZED

In Chapter 1, we discuss tech's tendency to become a little too enthusiastic—investors often bet huge sums of money on outlandish start-ups that need a miracle to succeed.

Afterward, in Chapter 2, we explore tech's obsession with growth. We'll see that many start-ups try to grow really quickly by using other people's money, so they're unprofitable for years. However, while such explosive growth is sometimes justified, it often doesn't pay off in the long run.

A lot of the money that funds tech's craze comes from venture capital. In Chapter 3, we discuss venture capital and reveal some worrying findings about it—venture capitalists often take a big cut of the money they manage for others even if their investments perform poorly. This may encourage them to try to invest as much money as possible instead of investing it judiciously, leading some people to compare the industry to a Ponzi scheme.

In Chapter 4, we examine the role of governments and central banks in the tech extravaganza. We'll see that innovative policies implemented after the 2008 crisis, such as quantitative easing, may have fueled the tech craze. In addition, governments sometimes give "free" money to tech start-ups, which start-ups don't have to return, making taxpayers foot their bills.

Chapter 5 explores the day-to-day work of techies. We discuss the epidemic of unproductivity which has been plaguing the sector, making many techies idle or busy working on menial tasks or unpromising products that will never be used. We talk about meetings, the Agile methodology, and the lean start-up, among other things.

Finally, in Chapter 6, I share my suggestions to improve the tech sector. I propose ways to prevent new waves of tech craze from rising over and over again. I also present ideas I hope can help techies and entrepreneurs work on more useful and promising stuff. It's important we all think about how to fix tech, or else we risk continuing to waste our valuable resources on doomed tech projects—and techies' iced matchas.

# CHAPTER 1

# MIRACLES

Back in the late 1990s, the rise of the internet caused an explosion of enthusiasm about the tech industry. Venture capitalists pumped more money than ever to help launch new technology start-ups, and unprofitable tech companies started selling their shares in open markets, promising they'd make immense profits in the future. The tech explosion had a large impact outside the field—people opened restaurants near tech hubs to feed hungry coders, travel agents expanded to book ever-increasing techies' business trips, and private individuals invested their life savings in shares of those yet-unprofitable tech companies. Even in my hometown, far from any tech hub, the local software engineering degree flourished, and every parent seemed to secretly—and not so secretly—wish their child would enroll in it. As with most economic booms, the impact of this tech extravaganza, now known as the *dot-com bubble*, was far-reaching.

In 2000, things took a dark turn. Tech companies didn't make their promised profits, so many of them went bust and hundreds of thousands of people lost their jobs—there were two hundred thousand layoffs in Silicon Valley alone.[1] Other sectors which had benefited from the boom suffered from collateral damage and, as the tech-heavy NASDAQ share marketplace tanked by 75%, many people lost a lot of money.

After such a dire experience, you'd think the world would become a bit more cautious about tech. However, if there was any caution, it didn't last long.

Throughout the 2010s, there was a new wave of enthusiasm about tech which dwarfed the dot-com bubble. This time, enthusiasm was largely driven by the remarkably fast growth of social networks and sharing economy start-ups like Uber and Airbnb. During this period, the sector received more money and became more extravagant than ever—by far. In the years between 2010 and 2020, the amount of money that venture capitalists poured into start-ups increased by a factor of nine; the sum went from $40 billion in 2010 to $342 billion in 2020. If that sounds dramatic already, brace yourself for what happened next.

Just a year later, in 2021, investors injected $681 billion into start-ups, *twice* the sum from the year before and a seventeen-fold increase from a decade earlier.[2] In 2021 alone, 787 start-ups reached *unicorn* status, meaning that investors considered them to be worth over one billion dollars when purchasing a portion of them. That is a rate of two new unicorns per day, higher than any other year in history and thirty times higher than a decade earlier.[3] Unicorns used to be a rare occurrence, hence the name, but in 2021 they became commonplace. Ten years before, there were twenty-two cities in the world with at least one unicorn in them; in 2021, there were 170.[4]

With so much cash in its coffers, the tech industry became

really extravagant. Entrepreneurs were given millions to experiment with outlandish business ideas that defeated all common sense. Tech offices became stylish, with beanbags and beer fridges, and employees were sent on team-bonding ski trips. I used to work for a tech company that hired an external entertainment provider to organize a scavenger hunt around the city for our delight. Some tech companies had so much cash that they hired talented employees just to prevent competitors from doing so, even if there was no work for them to do.[5] As usual, the economic boom affected many other industries, from restaurants located near tech hubs to producers of beanbags and organizers of scavenger hunts. No one was immune to the effects of the tech extravaganza.

This period of frenzy seemed a little too familiar to the dot-com bubble. In 2016, a survey of venture capitalists revealed that 91% of them thought unicorns were overvalued.[6] Even respondents who had invested in unicorns themselves agreed with that observation. In 2018, a tech strategist warned, "Silicon Valley tech bubble is larger than it was in 2000, and the end is coming."[7]

Note that some of *your* money is routinely used to fund the repeated episodes of tech frenzy. A lot of the money invested in tech comes from venture capital funds, or *VCs*, which are firms that decide how to invest other people's money in other people's businesses. VCs raise some of their money from universities, pension funds, and the government.[8] So, a part of your university tuition, pension pot and taxes are funneled toward VCs, and then it goes from there into tech. Whether you like it or not, you've most likely indirectly helped fund an entrepreneur's outlandish start-up idea or, perhaps, a techie's scavenger hunt.

Right after the record-breaking year of 2021, things took a dark turn. As central banks increased the cost of borrowing money and start-ups didn't grow as much as expected, there was a dramatic crash. In 2022, a few prominent tech companies announced massive layoffs. Then, other companies followed suit. Then the first ones announced even more layoffs, and then the other ones did the same. The phenomenon continued into 2023. After several rounds of layoffs, Amazon let go twenty-seven thousand employees, Microsoft ten thousand and Meta twenty-one thousand.[9] And that's just the tip of the iceberg—Dropbox, Yahoo, Spotify, Dell, Zoom, PayPal, Salesforce, Coinbase, Vimeo, GitHub, and Indeed each let go 5–20% of their staff. The most dramatic case was that of Twitter, which let go 75% of its workforce (six thousand employees) and even more later on. Similar layoffs took place at other tech companies which were less known to the general public, such as Waymo and Twilio. Many early-stage start-ups also laid off a large portion of their staff.[10]

Investment in the sector declined dramatically. In 2022, it was down by 35% compared to the record-breaking year of 2021. Some remained optimistic, as investment still remained quite high. But then, in 2023, it declined a further 50%, crushing optimism. The rate of appearance of new unicorns collapsed, from two a day in 2021 to three a month in 2023. The downfall of tech was deeply felt outside the sector too, as the now cash-deprived tech companies reduced their spending on others' products and services.

We're still in the middle of the turmoil as I write this, so we don't know what will happen next. But if it's anything like the past, we might end up forgetting about all this and slowly walk back into the next tech bubble.

Some may argue that the recurring waves of enthusiasm about tech are ultimately beneficial to society, as tech companies build new things and push the boundaries of innovation along the way, but I'm not sure that's what really happens. In this chapter, we'll look into whether the immense efforts and money—some of it *your* money—used to support tech's activities tend to be allocated in a sensible and useful way. We'll first talk about start-ups and then three common ways in which people become a little too enthusiastic and bet on start-ups that require a miracle to succeed.

## START-UPS

*Start-ups,* which are cherished by investors and entrepreneurs, are companies that seek to grow explosively. They try to expand at lightning speed and capture the largest possible market share as early as they can. Entrepreneur Paul Graham tells us:

> A startup is a company designed to grow fast. Being newly founded does not in itself make a company a start-up. Nor is it necessary for a start-up to work on technology, or take venture funding, or have some sort of "exit." The only essential thing is growth.[11]

While that's a fair description, we must also add that most start-ups not only want to grow fast, but they also want to grow big. Otherwise, investors and entrepreneurs don't bother much with them; they want a piece of a large pie, not a small one. That's why so many start-ups try to disrupt an entire industry or change the way many people live—they want to be the next Uber or Airbnb—and that's also why so many focus on potentially groundbreaking technology like artificial intelligence, blockchain, and the metaverse.

While a start-up does not necessarily develop a software product, the vast majority of them do. This is because software is particularly well placed to grow explosively, which is difficult to achieve with other types of products. Selling physical products, for example, is hard to scale because producing each extra unit of a physical product is costly. Selling services doesn't scale fast either, as the company needs to hire more and more employees to deliver its services as it grows.

Software is different. Once a piece of software is written, say, Spotify's music player, it can be distributed to many users with negligible additional cost and effort. That is especially true when the software is hosted centrally and provided to users via the web browser or apps (think of Spotify, Netflix, and Uber). In that case, users don't need heavy-duty equipment to use the product, which makes it very easy to access, and software updates reach all users immediately. This model, known as software as a service—or SaaS—has become investors' favorite. A friend joked, "If you want to get attention from investors, just say you're building a SaaS start-up. Even a bathroom management SaaS or something like that will do."

Start-ups usually raise money from investors to help them get started and grow. The word "investor" often means a person or institution deciding how to allocate other people's money, not their own. Traditionally, investing in start-ups is a risky endeavor because these companies suffer from a lot of uncertainty. One source of uncertainty is the market's response to the product: "Will customers like our product, use it, and pay for it?" Another source of uncertainty is technical unknowns: "Will we be able to build the product easily, and will there be unexpected blockers?" Because of the high-risk nature of the business, investors take pride in how careful and selective they are when giving money to start-ups. However, as we'll see next, their choices are often quite surprising.

## MARKET MIRACLES

Back in 2014, a twenty-year-old law graduate from the U.K. noticed that a lot of his peers worried about money and that many of them didn't like their banks.[12] So, he decided to launch an innovative digital bank targeted to students and millennials. The bank's app would address the needs of the young generation by offering tools to help them build budgets, track their spending, and save money.

The bank, called Loot, received seed money from the businessman who'd created Charles Tyrwhitt, a popular British brand specialized in suits and shirts. Thanks to this helpful nudge, Loot's team quickly put together a first version of the app. The founder explained, "We have a current account which works like a traditional bank account, but on top of that we have built loads of tech to help you manage your money. This includes things like live budgeting so you know exactly how much you can spend, free currency exchange abroad, or our 'goals feature' designed to help you put money aside and save. We try to focus our users on how much they can spend today, which is why our budgeting circle is the biggest thing you see when you open the app."[13] Down the line, Loot intended to make money the usual way banks do, by offering "products in lending, wealth management, and foreign exchange."

Loot faced a significant challenge: As with most banking start-ups, it was very hard to make the numbers add up because costs were high, and revenue was low. Start-ups like Loot cannot conduct their own banking operations, like issuing cards and opening accounts, because obtaining the required banking license costs tens of millions and takes years. So, they have to hire a third-party, licensed bank to do those tasks for them. This still gets very expensive very fast, as third-party providers charge high monthly subscriptions—in the tens of thousands—plus extra fees for each current account they hold. Some providers even charge a penalty if account holders don't use their debit cards often enough. So, the costs of running a digital bank are eye-wateringly high.

At the same time, the revenue collected per customer tends to be extremely low. As a rule of thumb, I was told digital banks require at least two million regular customers to even dream of breaking even. As Loot's target audience was cash-deprived students, it was probably even harder to squeeze revenue out of them. Moreover, some of Loot's intended revenue-generating products, such as wealth management services, didn't seem well suited to students.

But perhaps Loot's greatest challenge was to make students and millennials interested in budgeting and spend tracking, which were the bank's main offerings. Many budgeting tools already existed at the time, and while some students used them, they didn't seem crazy about them. My intuition also tells me that students don't usually care all that much about budgets. I was a short-of-cash student myself when Loot was launched, and so were most of my peers, but I don't recall any of us being interested in creating budgets or tracking our spending—we just tried to minimize our expenses across the board by cycling everywhere (even in bad weather), always eating in, and so on. Loot would also face fierce competition from traditional banks that already offered budgeting tools; while these tools weren't very user-friendly at the time, they could be quickly improved to challenge Loot if necessary.

With high costs, low revenue, a tepid market, and fierce competition, the only thing that could make Loot work as a business, and especially one that would reward investors handsomely, was a *market miracle*. Students would have to start caring about budgets all of a sudden and love Loot so much that they would quit their current banks and flock to it, and competitors would have to keep offering subpar tools that didn't match Loot's capabilities. Loot's cash-deprived clientele would have to generate unexpectedly high revenue by using their debit cards a lot and getting loans. The start-up would also have to grow and generate revenue very fast, or else the high bills of running it would quickly eat investors' money. The odds of all of this happening were extremely slim.

The need for a market miracle didn't deter investors. In 2016, the start-up raised £1.5 million from an Austrian venture capital firm, called Speedinvest, and a German one, called Global Founders Capital. Later that year, it raised another £2.5 million from the same investors.

By 2017, the bank managed to onboard fifty thousand customers. While this was a great achievement, it was still very short of the two million usually required to turn it into a viable business. Monthly bills became prohibitively high; they soon reached half a million pounds a month. (I told you running a bank was expensive.) Loot's *runway*, as it's often called, was really short, meaning that the company wouldn't be able to survive too long without another injection of cash from the outside. The £4 million that Loot had raised from investors soon evaporated.

Luckily for Loot, VCs came to the rescue. A Canadian fund owned by Power Corporation and other funds gave Loot £2.2 million. This only helped extend its lifetime by four months or so, but investors seemed eager to wait and see if the market miracle happened within that timeframe.

As months passed, Loot kept growing at a moderate pace, but it entered the red again. In 2018, a venture division of Royal Bank of Scotland came to the rescue by investing £3 million in the company. With such high expenses, the money didn't last long, so Royal Bank of Scotland gave Loot another £2 million six months later, in early 2019, helping extend its lifetime a few more months.

As time went by, the miracle everyone was praying for didn't happen. Loot had reportedly opened two hundred thousand current accounts, but customers didn't seem that enthusiastic about the bank's features and didn't use their debit cards much. Instead of the intended budgeting tools within the app, the most appealing feature to students was that it was easy to open an account with Loot compared to other banks. But that feature also attracted fraudsters, and Loot found itself with an unusually high number of fraudulent transactions to deal with.

By May 2019, just five months after the latest investment round, Loot had almost run out of cash again. It had enough money to survive another two months or so. The start-up was led to believe it would receive a new round of investment or, perhaps, be acquired by Royal Bank of Scotland. This didn't happen, and the company went bust. One of the lawyers in charge of its liquidation explained, "While the Loot offering is one that has attracted a lot of interest and praise, the business wasn't yet generating sufficient revenues to meet its ongoing costs and unfortunately the board could not secure the additional funding needed."[14] This outcome wasn't unexpected; in fact, it was, by far, the most likely one.

Loot's story illustrates a pronounced tendency that has taken over the tech world: the investment in market miracles. Investors have become extremely comfortable with betting on businesses that have all odds against them hoping that the market will react surprisingly well. As many of these early-stage start-ups only receive a few million in investment, it doesn't seem like a big deal in the grand scheme of things. However, early-stage investment makes up 40% of VC investment, or $200 billion in 2021. Sometimes, the investment in market miracles reaches huge proportions and can be quite comical.

In 2013, a Manhattan-based entrepreneur who'd run a chain of juice bars launched a start-up called Juicero. The company would build a high-tech, Wi-Fi-enabled fruit pressing machine to make juice at home. Much like Nespresso, users would have to purchase single-use capsules filled with pieces of fruit, which they'd insert in the machine.

The fancy apparatus would sell for a whopping price of $699, which was lower than the cost of manufacturing it.[15] Each capsule, which would cost $5–7, would have a lifespan of eight days, and the machine would verify its validity by reading a QR code printed on it. Juicero's founder called himself the Steve Jobs of juicing.[16]

Over the next three years, investors handed Juicero the staggering sum of $120 million to help it develop and launch its product. Investors included Kleiner Perkins, one of the most prestigious and oldest venture capital firms in the world.

Kleiner Perkins was the first VC to open an office on Sand Hill Road, a Silicon Valley artery famous for its concentration of venture capitalists. Another notable investor was Google Ventures, a VC arm of the internet giant.

The main challenge for Juicero was that the market for the product wasn't credible. Who would want to pay $699 for a juice presser, plus $5–7 for each glass of juice made by the machine? The idea defied common sense so much that some people thought it was an April Fool's prank.[17]

Investors hoped for a very big miracle here. Some wished Juicero would somehow turn into the Nespresso of juice. However, this ignored the obvious differences between the two. Making espresso requires expensive equipment because water has to be pumped at a very high pressure. Pressing juice is much simpler and doesn't require such specialized equipment. Moreover, Nespresso machines and their capsules were much cheaper than Juicero's.

When Juicero launched in March 2016, sales numbers were very low—the market miracle didn't happen. Six months later, the CEO stepped down and a former president of Coca-Cola North America took his place. Hoping to increase sales, in early 2017, he decided to reduce the price of the presser from $699 to $399. But people didn't seem eager to pay $399 for the device either, so sales remained low. Moreover, users started to report that they could just press the fruit capsules with their hands and obtain similar juice to the one produced by the machine.[18]

In July 2017, the CEO declared, "The current prices of $399 for the press and $5–7 for produce packs are not a realistic way for us to fulfill our mission at the scale to which we aspire." As the company was losing four million dollars a month, he announced the layoff of 25% of its employees.[19] Two months later, Juicero went bust. The start-up has been described as "the greatest example of Silicon Valley stupidity"[20] and an "absurd Silicon Valley startup product that raised huge funds but didn't really solve any real problem."[21] It's not clear investors saw it that way; many said they felt "Juicero was a victim of an anti-elitist political and media climate."[22]

I recently told an investor I was worried about how often start-ups seemed to receive money to build products that had all odds against them. He explained to me that his role as an investor was to support companies that faced market uncertainty: "If founders knew that there was a strong market for a certain product, then they could just go to the bank and ask for a loan." He added that by supporting start-ups that faced market uncertainty, he facilitated innovation.

It's true that there's always a chance that the market may not react to a new product as well as one would hope. In fact, this has historically been one of the most frequent causes of start-up failure.[23] Paul Graham tells us, "It sounds obvious to say you should only work on problems that exist. And yet by far the most common mistake start-ups make is to solve problems no one has."[24]

However, it seems that instead of supporting products that "could go either way," investors tend to support products that will probably go one way—failure—unless a miracle happens. When investors support companies like Loot or Juicero, there isn't much uncertainty about the outcome; instead, there are very high odds, even almost complete certainty, that the response will not be good enough to turn the start-up into a viable business.

There's a sentiment that this kind of hopeful investment became particularly common during the record-beating tech boom of the early 2020s. Technology reporter Hasan Chowdhury said, in 2022, "Lately, few ideas have proven to be too dumb for venture capital money."[25] This sentiment was also present in the aftermath of the dot-com bubble; back in 2001, professor of business administration D. Quinn Mills said, "Yes, the capital markets did a great job of channeling money into the new business sector that the dot-coms represented. But they did a lousy job of selecting which start-ups to support."[26]

## TECHNICAL MIRACLES

BenevolentAI is a British technology start-up that seeks to disrupt the pharmaceutical industry. Its goal is to speed up the development of new drugs. This process is usually very slow because new drug candidates must go through lengthy clinical trials to assess their safety and efficacy. Moreover, many candidates don't pass the trials, so significant efforts often lead nowhere.

The start-up promised to alleviate this problem with artificial intelligence. They argued that AI could "outperform human scientists in understanding the cause of disease" and be "capable of quickly generating drug candidates at scale."[27] Their AI-generated drug candidates, they argued, would have "a higher probability of clinical success than those developed using traditional methods."[28]

Thanks to its compelling promise, BenevolentAI secured $87 million in funding in 2015. In 2018, it raised a further $115 million and was valued at over $2 billion, thus officially becoming a unicorn. A year later, in 2019, it raised another $90 million. In 2021, shares of BenevolentAI started to be traded in the Euronext Amsterdam stock exchange.

The thing is, no one really knows if AI can achieve what BenevolentAI promised. In fact, no method yet exists that can do that. On this matter, drug discovery specialist Derek Lowe explained:

> I'm not sure at all if AI is ready to help across the board with that problem because that would imply that we have enough data and we need help interpreting it. And while we could certainly use such help, I think that the bigger problem is that we just don't know enough about cells, about organisms, and about disease. AI is going to be very good at digging through what we've already found, and the hope is that it'll tell us, from time to time, "Hey guys, you're sitting on something big here but you just haven't realized it yet". But producing new knowledge is something else.[29]

Despite skepticism, BenevolentAI tried to develop an AI-based proprietary method for drug discovery, and it used it to propose a handful of new drugs. A drug meant to treat dermatitis, called BEN-2293, became its flagship AI-discovered drug. In 2023, the outcome of a clinical trial for BEN-2293 was expected with high enthusiasm; a news website published an article entitled "BenevolentAI on the cusp of greatness."[30]

The drug didn't pass the test.[31] While it proved safe, it was no better than a placebo at treating dermatitis. A month later, the company announced it would let go half of its employees and cut spending on drug discovery programs.[32]

As AI-based drug discovery didn't prove fruitful, the start-up decided to divert its efforts to develop "a new suite of AI products, including a natural language biomedical querying system."[33] This probably meant that the start-up would develop a chatbot. The company's share price dropped by 90%.

BenevolentAI is just one of the many tech start-ups that are launched—and funded—to develop a product that nobody knows how to build. I recently attended the Paris Air Show, a trade show where aerospace companies present their products. There was a flashy corner that drew a lot of attention from the media and visitors. It was devoted to start-ups producing futuristic aircraft known as *eVTOLs,* which are electric passenger helicopters—or "flying cars." The aircraft on display seemed fully built, and attendees were taking turns to sit inside their cabins. The star of the show was an eVTOL named Midnight, designed by a Silicon Valley start-up called Archer.

Archer's promise is to launch a comprehensive service of air taxis around cities in the near future, based on its Midnight aircraft. Its air taxi service will offer rides for the same price as Uber Black (Uber's premium service).[34] The company has promised to someday add a thousand new air taxis every year.[35]

There's a catch though: None of the aircraft on display in the show could fly—they were all mock-ups. Archer's prototype, for example, had never been airborne, and its intended first flight had been delayed many times. Two months after the Paris show, an aircraft produced by one of Archer's main rivals, British start-up Vertical Aerospace, crashed during a test flight.[36]

In reality, as I write this, no one knows yet how to build a safe and effective eVTOL. The most important impediment is the weight of batteries. For an eVTOL to fly even a moderate distance, it would require batteries that are too heavy to lift off.

Even if some prototypes managed to take off, it's not clear whether they would be commercially viable due to their limited range and low payload. For example, Archer's proposed air taxis would be able to carry four passengers with hand luggage, but there would be no capacity for, say, a suitcase. Because of their limited range, the batteries of Archer's air taxis would have to be recharged for a few minutes between flights.[37]

Regulation might also be a problem, as the vehicles' design will need to be certified by the relevant authorities, such as the Federal Aviation Administration. The process is usually lengthy and, because eVTOLs are a new thing, it could be even lengthier than usual. Moreover, certifying the design of the aircraft is not enough; a separate certification is needed to be allowed to conduct commercial air operations. Many eVTOL start-ups have repeatedly promised to launch their air taxi services "within a year," but that timeframe is not realistic considering the stringent regulations and the fact that their aircraft can't fly yet. Maybe the future of mobility will change thanks to air taxis. As of today, however, there isn't a clear roadmap to achieve that.

The various challenges haven't deterred investors. Archer alone has received $450 million in investment so far.[38] What is even more surprising is that, in 2022, a first *vertiport* was inaugurated in Paris. This is a facility designed to handle air taxi operations. It includes landing pads and a small passenger terminal with check-in and security areas.[39] Soon after, the construction of five more vertiports started, funded through a combination of government and private money. The goal was to complete them in time for the 2024 Olympic Games so that attendees could use them, but it was unlikely that the vertiports would be used during the Olympics because there was almost zero chance that an air taxi would become operational, let alone certified, by then. In early 2024, just five months before the Olympics, air taxi companies and regulators acknowledged it wouldn't happen.[40]

There is always some technical uncertainty when building a start-up's product, just like with any engineering project. It's hard to know in advance exactly how hard building the product could be or which unexpected roadblocks may pop up. But there is one characteristic of BenevolentAI, eVTOLs and many other similar start-ups that sets them apart from the usual engineering project: they require a *discovery*. BenevolentAI, for example, requires discovering a new type of AI with unprecedented capabilities, and eVTOLs require discovering a new, lighter, and more compact way of storing electrical power. On the latter, reporter Eric Johansson tells us, "Companies around the world are working double-time to build new and better batteries—for instance, by trying to find new chemical compounds to replace the common lithium-ion ones used today—capable of storing more power. However, until that research bears fruit, flying cars are likely to remain a moonshot fantasy."[41]

It is tempting to think that discoveries can be "bought" by hiring many engineers and putting them in a room for long enough to try to solve the problem, but that's usually not the case. If it were the case, BenevolentAI would have succeeded in its quest for AI-discovered drugs, and air taxis would be flying all over major cities. Investors sometimes say, "It's just a matter of time until…" but if it were just a matter of time, how come so many coveted discoveries haven't been made despite devoting billions to them for many years?

Self-driving cars are a stellar example of how discoveries cannot be bought. Self-driving cars keep getting confused when they encounter unusual situations, and fixing this would require the discovery of a new AI approach that is more robust to unusual scenarios. That technology hasn't been discovered yet, even after $200 billion was invested in the industry. So, until today, the closest attempts to self-driving cars can only drive themselves within certain areas at certain times of the day and still get confused in unusual environments. Uber tried hard to develop self-driving cars, but the efforts were fruitless. One of its investors said, "We probably burned $2.5 billion on autonomous cars that was a waste of money."[42] If it was just a matter of injecting cash, we would probably have self-driving cars everywhere by now.

In reality, discoveries tend to be made in a pretty random way. Einstein formulated the special theory of relativity in his spare time while employed at the patent office, and Fleming discovered penicillin accidentally after mold grew inside a Petri dish. Sometimes multiple research labs try to solve a problem for years, and another one takes on the challenge much later and finds the solution quickly. Who knows which kind of improvement over batteries will make air taxis possible? And who knows where that discovery will be made?

Start-ups have become used to promising to build the final thing—the air taxi offering trips at Uber-like rates—without acknowledging that missing discoveries prevent that from happening. By not acknowledging the real difficulties, only a *technical miracle* can save them. As these miracles don't happen very often, many of these start-ups end up in disappointment or failure. They also miss opportunities to make actual progress in the intended area. For example, Uber's main motivation to develop self-driving cars was that it was operating at a loss and hoped these cars would help it make a profit. If it had acknowledged the task's real difficulty, perhaps it would've focused more on honing its existing business model.

This isn't to say that research is worthless because discoveries aren't guaranteed—discoveries have to be made somewhere, and it's worth looking. But there's a difference between doing research on a tough problem and pretending that the problem doesn't exist.

## PEOPLE MIRACLES

In 2018, a high-profile entrepreneur launched a start-up to revolutionize the world of video streaming. It was initially called NewTV but was soon rebranded as Quibi, which stands for "quick bits." The entrepreneur had been the co-founder and CEO of DreamWorks, known for *Shrek, Madagascar*, and other successful movies. He appointed as CEO an equally high-stakes executive who'd been at the head of eBay for ten years and had also worked in the entertainment industry at Disney and DreamWorks.

Quibi's goal was to create a mobile-only streaming service for millennials. It would offer a library of bite-sized videos like the ones found on TikTok but produced by high-profile, Hollywood crews. So, it would stand somewhere in between TikTok and Netflix. Its videos would last ten minutes and users would have to pay a monthly subscription to access the content.

Many people were highly skeptical that there was a market for this idea. Months before Quibi's launch, a Forbes article said:

> Quibi skeptics simply don't buy the service's fundamental premise—that more traditional Hollywood-style programming featuring Hollywood-style talent and production values will effectively translate to a mobile, millennial-driven audience. Do millennials care about A-list "brands" like Academy Award-winning directors Guillermo Del Toro and Peter Farrelly signing on to create exclusive premium content for the service? Will that kind of traditional Hollywood name-dropping matter?[43]

A Hollywood insider commented, "If I'm going to watch *Game of Thrones* in eight-minute chunks, what's the difference between what Quibi is doing and me hitting the pause button?"[44]

Despite skepticism, Quibi didn't do research to validate the market. They did not try out a prototype or create test content to see if it resonated with its intended audience. Investors didn't seem too bothered by this lack of due diligence, most likely because they were impressed by the team leading the company. Quibi raised the staggering sum of—brace yourself—$1.75 billion. That was even before it had a product, let alone a client. The company spent $1.1 billion on the creation of original content, including a show that cost a whopping $100,000 a minute to produce.[45]

The consensus was, however, that this was a large-scale experiment. Commentators acknowledged that it could go either way. The former CEO of Paramount Pictures called it a "bet" and said, "It's a giant and gutsy speculation. Most people when they hear it aren't overwhelmed by the idea, which makes it all the gutsier."[46]

In order to generate buzz, Quibi spent tens of millions on advertising campaigns before its launch. However, a heavy disconnect with its intended audience became evident in these campaigns. For example, they advertised the product at the Oscars, whose median viewer age is fifty-six. And their Super Bowl ad spent most of its thirty seconds trying to explain what the product was, instead of showcasing samples of the content to potential viewers. According to some reports, 70% of Super Bowl viewers thought Quibi was a food delivery app.[47]

When Quibi launched, its content wasn't well received. Most of its critics didn't appreciate the platform's video format. An article on *The Guardian* said it provided "a big pile of unnecessary stuff that's digested as quickly as it's forgotten."[48] A couple of weeks later, a *Vulture* article said that Quibi's shows "almost universally felt cheaper and less memorable than similar stuff on other platforms."[49] Its most definitive verdict, however, came from users. On launch day, the app reached third place in Apple's App Store. Two months later, it dropped to position 284.[50]

Some people argued that the COVID pandemic didn't help, as people were commuting much less, so the need for watching short videos on their phones wasn't as pronounced. However, TikTok's popularity soared during COVID lockdowns,[51] so this argument doesn't seem watertight.

Quibi had predicted seven million paid subscribers within its first year. Six months after launch, it only had five hundred thousand.[52] By then, the company had only collected $3.3 million in subscription fees, against over a billion spent on creating content, and revenue had started to trend downward.[53]

Because of its poor adoption, Quibi shut down six months after it was launched. In a public announcement, the founding team explained:

> Quibi is not succeeding. Likely for one of two reasons: because the idea itself wasn't strong enough to justify a standalone streaming service or because of our timing. Unfortunately, we will never know but we suspect it's been a combination of the two. The circumstances of launching during a pandemic is something we could have never imagined but other businesses have faced these unprecedented challenges and have found their way through it. We were not able to do so.[54]

The statement explained, "As entrepreneurs our instinct is to always pivot, to leave no stone unturned—especially when there is some cash runway left—but we feel that we've exhausted all our options. As a result, we have reluctantly come to the difficult decision to wind down the business, return cash to our shareholders, and say goodbye to our colleagues with grace." The company had $350 million left to return to investors, having spent 80% of all the cash that had been given by them.[55]

As is often the case with start-ups, some of the money invested in Quibi indirectly came from the general public. For example, one investor was Future Fund, a taxpayer-owned organization that manages billions on behalf of the Australian government. According to its website, the fund's goal is "to invest for the benefit of future generations of Australians."[56] It invested $50 million in Quibi.[57]

Investors take pride in following a carefully designed

playbook that helps them minimize risk. One of the main tenets of the playbook is that start-up investment should be done one step at a time. Instead of giving a lot of money to a start-up in one go, there should be multiple rounds of investment tied to objectives; only when an objective is attained is another round of investment unlocked. So, we often hear of *pre-seed* and *seed* investments, which are relatively small lump sums—rarely over a million—meant to help a start-up get off the ground. When a start-up proves some interest in its product, even if it's not finished and far from perfect, it raises a new round called *Series A*, of around ten million, meant to help it build a more established business. This is followed by *Series B, Series C*, and so on, usually of $50 million or more each time, which are meant to help the company grow at an explosive rate. The key at each step is to validate a hypothesis, for example, by proving that people love the product or that clients remain subscribed for a long time.

The case of Quibi, however, shows that investors don't always follow their own playbook. In this case, they abandoned their step-by-step approach by giving Quibi $1.75 billion in one go. They also did away with any validation of the customer's interest in the product. Had they validated the idea with potential customers, argues a product manager, "They would have had people asking why Quibi when they have TikTok, Instagram, and YouTube for free when they're on the toilet. And why Quibi when they are paying for Netflix and Prime already."[58] The main reason—or perhaps excuse—to abandon the playbook was that the founders had impressive careers.

Perhaps a start-up known as Mistral will suffer the same fate. Mistral is a French start-up launched in June 2023. Mistral's goal is to become a major European competitor to the AI powerhouse OpenAI. In a strategy memo, the start-up explained, "All major actors are currently US-based, and Europe has yet to see the appearance of a serious contender."[59]

Other than that, Mistral didn't define what it would do. In the memo, the company promised to do something within generative AI that would be "much better than currently available products" thanks to the use of "high-quality data content," but no concrete product was proposed. They also promised to provide "unmatched guarantees on security and privacy," without specifying how.[60]

The business model wasn't clear either. In order to make money, Mistral's memo suggested it would reserve its strongest and most specialized AI "for negotiated access." However, it also suggested it would differentiate itself from competitors by being open and letting the world see the internal details of how its technology works. Mistral suggested a few other vague ways to make money, such as "partnering with integrators/consulting companies to establish commercial contracts for fully integrated solutions." The memo also said, "We will explore and identify the best [business] approach in parallel to technological development."[61]

With such a rough proposal, you'd think nobody would invest in Mistral. However, it raised the staggering sum of €103 million from a handful of VCs and the French government.[62] The main reason Mistral raised so much money without a real product or business plan was the impressive credentials of its founders; they had all specialized in AI and knew each other since college, and one of them used to work for Google's DeepMind while the other two used to work for Meta. A fund manager who led the investment said, "There's a pool of eighty to one hundred people globally who have the level of experience they have."[63] He added that running an AI start-up requires a lot of money in terms of computing power and top-tier talent, hence the need for such a large up-front investment. For months, Mistral's website only said, "We're assembling a world-class team to develop the best generative AI models," and it had a link to a list of job openings.

Just like with Quibi, the investors of Mistral decided that it was okay to bypass the usual due diligence. Once again, they argued that it was the amazing background of the people involved in the start-up that allowed them to do that—they hoped for people miracles. Perhaps Mistral will succeed in its quest, but that doesn't turn this investment into a responsible one.

Quibi and Mistral are "innocent" examples of how the bar of due diligence has become quite low as of late. In some cases, however, investors have repeatedly poured money into fraudulent start-ups. The most famous examples are those of Theranos and FTX, which received $724 million and $1.8 billion from investors, respectively, and were uncovered as deeply fraudulent later on. A former FTX employee said, "Think about the investors that invested in FTX, with access to all the documents they could ever want about the company's financials, and they still poured hundreds of millions of dollars into this enterprise."[64] A common explanation was, once again, that investors became enchanted by the founders' profiles. Regarding the founder of FTX, for example, professor of American history Margaret O'Mara said, "His wearing cargo shorts on stage with Tony Blair and Bill Clinton, the kind of really performative sloppiness that he had was, I think, part of the story. It was irresistible to everyone who was watching it."[65]

The immense amount of cash injected into tech during the latest boom may have come at the expense of a lowering of the bar of due diligence. Reporter Brooke Masters explained, "Veteran Silicon Valley dealmakers say there has been a gradual erosion of standards, as venture capitalists stopped trying to select and nurture the smartest entrepreneurs and started spraying cash around."[66]

I asked a venture capitalist whether he thought investors were conducting enough due diligence. He told me, "Look at the cases of Theranos and FTX. When you find a cockroach in your kitchen, there's one thing you don't want to ask but know the answer to: Are there others?"

## THE CONSEQUENCES

The tendency to invest in miracles has some unpleasant consequences. For starters, it is a source of immense unhappiness to a lot of employees. Many people join a tech company thinking they'll build something useful that will be ultimately used by others—and that's how the job is advertised to them. After working there for a while, they realize that the intended product has obvious flaws and only a miracle can save it. Ideally, the start-up would pivot away from that product at some point, but that doesn't happen all that often in practice. As a result, morale soon runs low in the company, and employees become frustrated or even idle.

Chasing miracles also takes talent away from genuinely useful projects. That's a pity, as there are so many industries that could be made more efficient with technology, but their problems are overlooked because they don't fit the start-up mold.

For example, an aerospace engineer showed me how commercial satellite companies use chaotic Excel spreadsheets to coordinate the ground logistics before launching a satellite. The spreadsheets often get lost or become outdated, which causes delays. Another engineer showed me how aircraft maintenance records are still kept on paper; this causes a lot of pain when a plane switches airlines, as the plane's owner needs to review all the records.

A cosmetics brand manager showed me how sales records from different department stores are all sent around by email in different formats, so it's hard to have good visibility of overall sales. If only talented techies were working on improving those outdated processes instead of developing a "millennial-focused banking product pitched at Generation Snapchat"[67] or a Wi-Fi-enabled juice presser.

And now let's talk about money. By investing in miracles, investors play a dangerous game with other people's money. Their hope is that when a miracle does happen for a start-up in their portfolio, it will outweigh the losses incurred by other start-ups. That is always a possibility, just like winning the lottery is. But does the strategy work well on average, in the long run? The evidence suggests that it doesn't—we'll come back to this point later—so it is likely that VCs are systematically making others worse off.

This is an issue for you because, if you remember, some of *your* money is used to fund these investments. Loot's largest investor, for example, was Royal Bank of Scotland, which committed five million British pounds to the start-up. The majority of Royal Bank of Scotland is owned by the British taxpayer. Notably, the bank received a 45-billion-pound rescue package from the government during the financial crisis of 2008.[68]

Across the channel, French taxpayers funded Mistral and footed the bill to build the illusory vertiports in time for the 2024 Olympics, on which no air taxi was likely to land. Across the Atlantic, the Ontario Teachers' Pension Plan, which pays the pension of 148,000 retired teachers, handed a check for $95 million dollars to fraudulent FTX. And the California Public Employees' Retirement System handed $300 million to a VC[69] which then handed $38 million to FTX.[70] Since then, the Californian pension fund has decided to *increase* its allocation to venture capital.[71] In Australia, taxpayer money helped fund the extravagant Quibi, and more and more countries are jumping onboard. An important Mexican pension fund, for example, devoted 100 million dollars to venture capital.[72] Wherever you look, money from the public—*your* money—is directly or indirectly used to fund VCs' miracle investments and support the tech extravaganza.

# CHAPTER 2

# EXPLOSIVE GROWTH

A few years ago, I had a job interview with a fast-growing start-up. At the end of the interview, the manager offered to answer questions, and I asked him how they intended to make a profit, as margins in their sector were really low and competition was fierce. He told me that their goal was to grow the company as fast as possible, and they'd think how to make a profit later on. "We're doing it the start-up way," he added.

The *start-up way* is to spend aggressively in order to grow really fast. This makes the start-up lose money for years, which is only possible thanks to the continued injection of cash from investors. For example, WeWork, the chain of co-working spaces, used investors' money to subsidize its prices and thus undercut competitors. The owner of a competing co-working space explained, "My average rate was $550 per desk per month, and I was just scraping by. Then WeWork arrived, and I had to drop it to $450, and then $350. It eviscerated my business."[1] The owner of another co-working space said, "*No one* could make money at these prices. But they kept lowering them so that they were cheaper than everyone else. It was like they had a bottomless bank account that made it impossible for anyone else to survive." This practice, which some see as predatory pricing,[2] helped WeWork grow very fast and expand internationally.

Start-ups also fuel their growth through lavish marketing campaigns. The start-up Peloton, for example, which produces high-tech exercise bikes, opened huge showrooms in upmarket streets around the world, including Madison Avenue in Manhattan and King's Road in London. And Quibi, the video streaming company, ran a costly ad at the Super Bowl. Start-ups also spend generously on continuously adding new features to their products even just to "test and learn" what users want.

If a start-up were to make a profit, it would be expected to spend every penny of it on more growth. While traditional businesses tend to distribute a part of their profits to owners, start-ups don't usually do that. In fact, investors can and will veto the distribution of profits.

Have a look at Spotify's bottom line (revenue minus spending), year after year since its inception:

| Year | Bottom line (millions of $) | Year | Bottom line (millions of $) |
| --- | --- | --- | --- |
| 2009 | −20 | 2017 | −1,396 |
| 2010 | −29 | 2018 | −92 |
| 2011 | −47 | 2019 | −208 |
| 2012 | −88 | 2020 | −664 |
| 2013 | −66 | 2021 | −40 |
| 2014 | −198 | 2022 | −453 |
| 2015 | −242 | 2023 | −576 |
| 2016 | −568 | | |

We can see that Spotify has lost money every year so far, sometimes in the hundreds of millions. This was possible thanks to the continued injection of cash from the outside. As of today, other famous unprofitable start-ups are Uber, Pinterest, Snapchat, Reddit, Fiverr, Lyft, Wayfair, Zillow, Eventbrite, DocuSign, Vroom, Twilio, Deliveroo, Palantir, and Robinhood. These have all lost money every year or almost every year since they were created.

The start-up model promises to reward patience under the belief that, if a start-up grows large enough, it will someday turn huge profits which will far outweigh previous losses. Business reporter Rani Molla explains, "Investors are willing to buy in now in order to subsidize and grow a company that could make lots of money later. They believe that the companies' future profits will eclipse these current losses. Let's call this the Amazon archetype. The retail giant has been notorious for taking in little profit relative to revenue in order to grow its business and invest in new initiatives for future profitability."[3]

Note that investors can still make a lot of money from an unprofitable start-up, provided that others believe in its future profitability. Suppose an unprofitable start-up goes public, meaning that it starts trading its shares in an open market like the New York Stock Exchange. Early investors may use that market to sell their shares; if others are convinced that the start-up will become profitable, they'll pay them good money for it.

Enthusiasm for unprofitable start-ups has reached monumental proportions. Back in 1980, only 10% of the tech companies that went public were unprofitable. In the 1990s, this figure skyrocketed. By the year 2000, in the height of the dot-com bubble, a whopping 85% of them were unprofitable.[4]

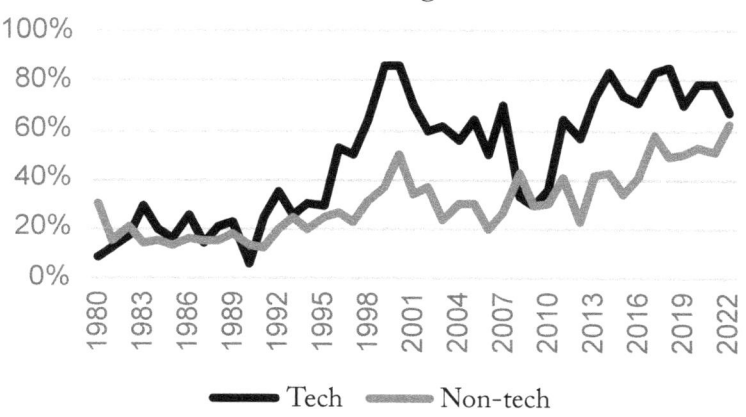

## Percentage of Unprofitable Companies When Going Public

*Tech — Non-tech*

As we can see in the above graph, after the dot-com bubble burst, enthusiasm for unprofitable tech companies went down. However, it still remained high compared to other sectors. After the financial crisis of 2008, it skyrocketed almost back to dot-com levels. It is safe to say that the vast majority of tech companies that go public are unprofitable. People trade their shares on the promise that they'll become profitable someday.

Following the success of companies like Amazon, the tech sector has adopted a grow-at-all-costs strategy. Becoming profitable, which is necessary to pay the bills in the long run, is deferred far into the future. In the meantime, losses keep piling up. But is this justified? In this chapter, we'll see that, despite the enormous enthusiasm for explosive growth, this only makes long-term sense under limited circumstances. And we'll see that many start-ups escape those circumstances, so in the long run their explosive growth on other people's dime doesn't pay off. We'll start by discussing entrepreneurs' greatest fear—copycats—and the solution to it: building a protective moat around the business. We'll then discuss how some start-ups fail to build moats, some drown in the moats of others, and some believe their moats are stronger than they are.

## COPYCATS

Lately, I've been renting electric bikes to move around London. These e-bikes are all over the city and you can pick one up on the street and drop it off somewhere else. The first e-bike company to set operations in London was Lime, a Silicon Valley start-up that raised a total of $1.5 billion in funding. The start-up negotiated deals with local authorities and deployed hundreds of bikes around the city in early 2019. Two years later, in 2021, a Dutch company called Dott, which raised over $100 million from investors, deployed a similar service in London. A year later, a British start-up called HumanForest launched a similar service, after raising $20 million from investors. And just two months after that, a company called Tier, which received over $600 million in investment, did the same. So, there is no shortage of e-bike start-ups in London. Sometimes I look out the window and see bikes from four different brands parked outside my building.

How do I choose which brand of e-bike to use? The e-bikes themselves are almost identical, and the user experience is very similar—even the phone apps used to unlock the bikes look the same across brands. You'd think I'd pick the cheapest one, but they've all tried to beat each other's offers, so their prices have dwindled to a similar level. There's no incentive for me to pick one brand over the other, let alone pay more for it.

This situation is typical of a highly competitive market, meaning that new companies can offer similar services and compete against existing ones on similar terms. When this happens, prices go down for everyone and no start-up can make sustained high profits. This is appreciated by consumers but not so much by businesses, especially the ones that promised huge returns to their investors.

Due to the highly competitive landscape, the London e-bike start-ups are already showing signs of strain. One of them, Tier, is said to be struggling,[5] and Dott shut down its e-bike service in September 2023, saying it was not possible to "run a financially sustainable" operation in London.[6]

Many people seem to believe that this unfortunate situation can be prevented by growing fast. Venture capitalist Jeffrey Housenbold explains, "Once Uber is founded, within a year you suddenly have three hundred copycats. The only way to protect your company is to get big fast by investing hundreds of millions."[7]

This line of thinking, however, is incorrect. Growing fast does *not* by itself protect a company from copycats. If copycats are able to enter the market on the same terms as their predecessors, they will do so and erode profits for everyone. If Lime, the first e-bike provider in London, had deployed its service even faster, this would have made little difference—other start-ups, backed by hundreds of millions in funding, would have still deployed their competing services a little bit later. Investors could have poured twice as many millions into Lime, and copycats would have still arrived and eroded its profits.

The only antidote to this situation is for a start-up to enjoy some sort of exclusive privilege that protects it from profit-eroding competitors. This kind of privilege is known as a *moat*, although it also goes by the names "competitive advantage," "barrier to entry," and even "monopolistic advantage." Perhaps one of the greatest sins of the start-up world is to downplay the importance of moats—*just pour a few hundred million into a company, grow it fast, and you'll be fine!*

## MOATS

In the 2000s, small hotels struggled to be found online by travelers, as the large booking websites like Priceline and Expedia only focused on big hotel chains. Things changed when a small online travel agency from the Netherlands came to the rescue. The agency went through the painstaking process of establishing relationships with small hotels, one by one, even from unpopular destinations, and listed them on its website. The chief marketing officer at the time later explained, "We focused on long-tail markets early on. We built inventory in secondary and tertiary destinations."[8] The online travel agency, known as Booking.nl, expanded fast and was soon rebranded Booking.com.

As Booking.com listed more and more hotels on its website, it became more and more appealing to travelers. At the same time, the more travelers used Booking.com, the more hotels were interested in listing their rooms there. So, as it grew, Booking.com took its customers captive. After a while, travelers didn't want to visit alternative websites, as they didn't find as many rooms there, and hotels didn't want to list their rooms on alternative websites because travelers didn't use them. Hotels were so captivated by Booking.com that they offered it preferential room rates in exchange for benefits like a "thumbs-up seal of approval."

When Booking.com grew, it served an untapped market, so it grew cheaply. A copycat would have to spend much more money to grow because it would have to convince people to migrate away from Booking.com to a new platform with fewer rooms and worse deals. This is a moat for Booking.com because a competitor would not be able to obtain the same results even if it imitated all its actions and spent as much money. This kind of moat is known as a *network effect*, and it happens when a product becomes more valuable to users the more users it has. This moat also protects social networks and online marketplaces.

Another popular way to build a moat is to make it inconvenient or expensive for users to switch to a different provider. For example, it's very easy to change iPhones; you just place the new phone next to the old one and all your data and customizations get transferred. In a matter of minutes, your new phone looks exactly like the old one. A competitor with an equally good product would struggle to convert iPhone users because making the switch would be much more inconvenient. This moat is known as a *switching cost*.

So far, we've discussed moats based on holding customers captive. In theory, it's also possible to build a moat by holding resources captive. The most important example of this is a patent, which grants a company exclusive access to an invention. However, patents are difficult to enforce, especially across borders, and have a limited duration. So, because resource-based moats aren't very strong, most successful tech companies rely on moats based on customer captivity, like network effects and switching costs, in order to defend their positions.

If you find the idea of moats a bit unpleasant, you're not alone. Consumers tend not to like moats all that much, as they reduce their options and increase prices. However, a moat is necessary to justify the explosive growth and sustained losses of start-ups. If a start-up spends millions of other people's money to grow fast, it'd better have a moat or a solid plan to build one! Otherwise, competitors will enter the market, dilute its profits, and all that spending on explosive growth will never be recuperated.

## NO MOAT? NO PROBLEM!

WeWork is a bankrupt chain of co-working spaces targeted at small businesses. It opened its first office in Manhattan in 2011. WeWork raised a whopping $21.7 billion from investors to grow explosively. The long list of investors included Harvard Management Company, which manages Harvard University's investments,[9] as well as a bunch of well-known VCs like SoftBank and Benchmark, and high-profile investment banks like Goldman Sachs and JPMorgan Chase. Thanks to its deep pockets and aggressive growth strategy, WeWork opened 779 locations in thirty-nine countries.

The start-up would one day have to ramp down its enormous spending on growth. That day, it wouldn't want competitors to steal its customers and erode its profits. Otherwise, why bother growing so rapidly in the first place? In other words, WeWork needed a moat. However, it was hard to imagine how it could build one—how could WeWork hold customers captive in a way that other co-working spaces couldn't? WeWork certainly offered great amenities, like beer taps, barista-made coffee, and ping-pong tables, but all of that could be easily offered by competitors.

WeWork tried to convince the world that it would build a moat based on network effects, just like Booking.com or LinkedIn. Its founder explained that it would become a "physical social network."[10] That's why WeWork ran social events inside the offices and referred to its tenants as "members." The company's website explained, "Our Community Team regularly hosts activities like networking, lunch-and-learns and more, plus fun activities to help add entertainment to the day." WeWork listed "professional and social events" as one of its amenities, on par with Wi-Fi and meeting rooms.[11]

To foster a sense of community, WeWork placed a community manager inside every office. One of them explained, "I once planned a *Friends*-themed trivia game for a member who was a superfan. We decorated the room and got buzzers so the participants could ring in their answers. It was so rewarding to see the joy and surprise on the member's face."[12] Other common activities included Easter egg hunts and ping-pong tournaments.[13]

To reinforce the idea that WeWork was building network effects, its founder instructed employees to describe the business as a "lifestyle or community-focused company" instead of a real-estate company.[14] An investor explained, "The pitch seems to be: come work here and you'll be with all these really good-looking young people that will help you do deals."[15]

WeWork's hope to build network effects was quite naïve because social interactions were limited geographically; a customer didn't get much value from WeWork growing fast in a different city, or even a different neighborhood. Moreover, a lot of "physical social networks" already existed. One of them was the pub, where workers hung out after work during happy hour. There also existed plenty of professional events and trade shows where small business owners interacted.

In 2019, the still unprofitable company sought to raise more funding by selling some its shares in a public market. This required filing a form describing the company with the U.S. Securities and Exchange Commission. In the absence of a credible moat, the company tried to describe itself as a technology business, as if that was enough to justify its ambitious and persistent quest for investment and growth. The language in the form was remarkably cryptic. Here's an excerpt:

> The entire member experience is powered by technology designed to enable our members to manage their own space, make connections among each other and access products and services, all with the goal of increasing our members' productivity, happiness and success. Technology is at the foundation of our global platform. Our purpose-built technology and operational expertise has allowed us to scale our core WeWork space-as-a-service offering quickly, while improving the quality of our solutions and decreasing the cost to find, build, fill and run our spaces.[16]

The word "technology" appeared 112 times in the document. This time, investors weren't convinced; when scrutinizing the form, it became clear to a lot of them that WeWork was a real-estate business that did not enjoy a moat like successful tech businesses did. WeWork had to infamously cancel its public offering, as it seemed that the demand for its shares would be extremely low. The day after, the founder resigned as CEO and was later awarded $245 million to cut all ties with the company.[17] A month after the failed public offering, WeWork promised to change course and have a more "disciplined focus on profitable market share expansion."[18]

WeWork continued growing over the following years. The COVID-19 pandemic hit it hard, but the occupancy of its offices recovered to pre-pandemic levels by August 2022.[19] However, the company still failed to turn a significant profit, let alone one that justified its outlandish spending on growth. In the absence of a moat, this was the most expected outcome. In November 2023, the start-up filed for bankruptcy.

Perhaps WeWork hoped to find an unexpected moat at some point. After all, opportunities for moats come and go as market conditions change, and a business must adapt its strategy over time. It is surprising, however, that investors were so hopeful this would happen that they gave WeWork nearly $22 billion.

## DROWNING IN THE MOAT

Hopper is a travel booking app that launched in 2014. The app initially focused on providing innovative tools to help users find cheap flights. For example, it included a color-coded calendar that let users easily visualize the cheapest travel dates. It also included a price prediction feature that sent a notification to the user when it deemed it was the best time to book a flight.[20] Enthusiastic investors gave Hopper $60 million to help it grow faster.[21]

The enthusiasm about Hopper was a bit surprising because the market was already crowded and strongly held by two gigantic companies with strong moats: Booking.com and

Expedia. Don't be fooled by the apparent variety of travel apps, as most of them are owned by either one of these two giants. (For example, Booking.com owns Priceline, Kayak, Momondo, and Agoda, among others, while Expedia owns Hotels.com, Orbitz, Travelocity, and Hotwire.com).

Hopper didn't know how it would make money, so it decided to go ahead "the start-up way." One of its executives explained, "One of the benefits of being a start-up is you don't have to have a revenue-generating model right away."[22] But the start-up soon realized that it would be very hard to make money by selling flights. This was because airlines had been trying to cut out intermediaries, so they paid very low to zero commission on flight sales. Instead, the real money was in hotels, where commissions were much higher. So, in 2017, Hopper added a hotel-booking feature to its app.

Selling hotel rooms is extremely hard for new travel apps because of the moats strongly held by Booking.com and Expedia. Hopper would have found it very difficult to sign deals with thousands of hotels individually because most of them were already held captive by the two giants. So, instead, Hopper decided to piggyback on Booking.com and Expedia. Hopper listed hotels from Booking.com and Expedia on its own app, sold their rooms to unsuspecting users, and earned an affiliate commission for it. This is what most independent travel booking apps do. For example, when an airline offers you to add a room to your flight reservation, the room secretly comes from Booking.com or Expedia, which pays the airline an affiliate commissions for sales.

Over the next few years, Hopper grew really fast thanks to investors' money, which gave Hopper a total of $727 million. In 2022, it became the most downloaded travel app in the

U.S. All this time, Hopper continued to piggyback heavily on Booking.com and Expedia's hotels.

Then the worst happened.

In July 2023, Expedia decided to cancel its affiliate partnership with Hopper, preventing the start-up from selling Expedia hotels to its customers. This severely reduced the number of hotels the start-up could offer on its app. Expedia's official reason for the move was that Hopper's features "exploited consumer anxiety and confused customers."[23] Hopper accused Expedia of making an "anti-competitive" move, which was a much more credible explanation. Perhaps the start-up should have been surprised at that point that Expedia let it piggyback on its hotel inventory for so long. But not all was lost: Hopper was still selling Booking.com's hotels. However, that didn't last.

Just three months after Expedia's debacle, Hopper pre-emptively stopped listing Booking.com's hotels. The start-up realized Booking.com would soon ban it, and it was more graceful to exit voluntarily. This resulted in a dramatically reduced offer of hotels on Hopper's app compared to a few months before. Two days later, Hopper laid off 30% of its employees.[24] The start-up was left with no choice but to rely on smaller hotel networks or establish direct relationships with hotels one by one—this was no easy feat. Time will tell how Hopper manages to reinvent itself.

The story of Hopper shows us that sometimes investors are happy to give money to start-ups whose intended customers are strongly protected by the moats of others, turning all odds against them. In this case, they gave over $700 million to Hopper, even though the start-up would have to fight against the moats already strongly held by others and then build a moat of its own. That was no easy task! When Booking.com and Expedia saw Hopper as a threat, they exercised the power of their moats to damage the start-up. Whether we like it or not, this was highly expected. It is unclear whether investors were unaware of the fight Hopper was up for, or they decided to invest in the start-up anyway, hoping for a miracle.

## MOAT ILLUSIONS

A start-up founder recently showed me his presentation slides to pitch his business idea to venture capitalists. The presentation included a list of moats enjoyed by the business. However, all of the moats in the list were great features of the product that would certainly be appreciated by customers, but they were not true moats that could protect the start-up from competitors in the long run. It has become common to consider too many things as moats. Economist Bruce Greenwald argues, "Contrary to popular management discourse, there are only a few types of competitive advantages, and examples of sustained competitive advantages in the business world are uncommon."[25]

In this section, we'll review three characteristics that are commonly touted as moats by tech companies, yet they aren't true moats or are not as powerful as they seem—they're moat illusions.

### *The 10x Illusion*

In November 2022, OpenAI launched its famous AI chatbot, ChatGPT, which gained 100 million users in just two months. This made ChatGPT the fastest adopted piece of software in history.[26] The reason for its success was very simple: It worked *much* better than any previous chatbots. Investors were so enthusiastic that they handed $10 billion to OpenAI right after ChatGPT was released.

The core of the technology behind ChatGPT was not invented by OpenAI; it was invented by a group of Google researchers five years before, who described it in an article in detail.[27] OpenAI adapted that methodology to create ChatGPT. Because the core of the technology is publicly known, other companies like Meta and Google soon launched their own competitors to the chatbot, and open-source alternatives also appeared.

In May 2023, a leaked Google memo said, "We have no moat and neither does OpenAI. … The uncomfortable truth is, we aren't positioned to win this arms race and neither is OpenAI. …While our AI still holds a slight edge in terms of quality, the gap is closing astonishingly quickly. Open-source AI is faster, more customizable, more private, and pound-for-pound more capable."[28] The memo also admitted, "We have no secret sauce," and it suggested, "People will not pay for restricted AI when free, unrestricted alternatives are comparable in quality. We should consider where our value add really is."

ChatGPT could be described as a "10x" product, an increasingly popular term used to describe technology that is at least ten times better than the previous one. A lot of people seem to believe that building a 10x product is a way to build a moat. Entrepreneur Peter Thiel explains, "As a good rule of thumb, proprietary technology must be at least 10 times better than its closest substitute in some important dimension to lead to a real monopolistic advantage."[29] The belief in the power of technical superiority has generated enormous interest in 10x start-ups. A venture capitalist explains, "A common question facing founders when pitching for VC investment is what makes your idea, product or business model 10x better than incumbents."[30]

Technological superiority, however, is *not* a moat. Unless the company has access to an exclusive resource to build that technology, then competitors will most likely catch up with it at some point, just like the Google memo explained.

Ideally, a company could protect its technology through secrecy. However, that's not a durable moat. For example, all the details of Meta's contender to ChatGPT were leaked to the public on a post on 4chan.org, a week after its release.[31] Moreover, unless a company has found a secret sauce that others won't be able to find, competitors can hire equally talented engineers to develop a similar product. Patents could also protect the superior technology in theory, but as they're not easy to enforce, they're rarely a true moat. In fact, Google holds a patent on the methodology that let OpenAI build ChatGPT,[32] but it hasn't enforced it, perhaps because it expects an ugly legal battle that would be hard to win.

Technological superiority, 10x or not, is an example of an illusory moat that has become all too popular. It is a nice and useful feature to have; for example, it can help kickstart a business and gain a first batch of enthusiastic customers. However, the company still needs to find a way to build a true moat, such as network effects or switching costs. In January 2024, for example, OpenAI launched a marketplace where people can buy and sell their own ChatGPT-based AI agents. This seemed like a focused attempt to build a network effect in the absence of other moats. We'll see how it goes.

*The Scale Illusion*

In 2022, Netflix spent a whopping $143 million to produce one season of *The Crown*, one of the most expensive TV shows in history. The sum sounds impressive, but it was only a drop in the bucket for Netflix. The streaming platform had grown so large at that point that the sum only represented 0.5% of its yearly revenue. If a small competitor wanted to produce a similar show, it would find spending $143 million much harder to fathom.

This situation arises when a cost is fixed, meaning that it's independent of the number of customers; it costs the same to produce *The Crown* to Netflix than to a smaller company. However, as Netflix is large, it can "spread the costs" across many sales. This situation is known as *economies of scale*.

As it's less painful for Netflix to spend $143 million than it is for a competitor, we get the impression that Netflix enjoys some sort of privilege. So, it has become fashionable to describe economies of scale as a type of moat. This idea has been promoted in countless books and blogs on business strategy, microeconomics, and entrepreneurship.[33]

Software companies enjoy particularly impressive economies of scale because writing software has a "one-off" cost independent of the number of users—you write it once and then distribute it to many users at almost no extra cost. Peter Thiel explains, "Software start-ups can enjoy especially dramatic economies of scale because the marginal cost of producing another copy of the product is close to zero."[34] As many people believe that economies of scales are a moat, they also believe that software start-ups, which tend to enjoy extreme economies of scale, can build a moat automatically just by growing large.

Economies of scale, however, is not a strong moat by itself because investors are more than happy to help a start-up grow at a loss until it reaches a favorable scale. If you remember, the streaming platform Quibi spent one billion dollars to produce videos before it even had a single user! It didn't matter to Quibi that it couldn't "spread the costs" among as many users as Netflix.

If investors think there is good opportunity in a certain market, they help start-ups grow to acquire a portion of that promising market. In the absence of a true moat, the market ends up splitting more or less evenly among all of the competitors.[35] If a large company wants to enjoy the benefits of superior economies of scale, it still needs a true moat, such as network effects or switching costs, to retain its market share. Being large is not enough.

Surprisingly, a *small* scale can be a powerful moat, contrary to what many investors and entrepreneurs seem to strive for. Imagine you run a start-up with $60 in fixed costs (rent, staff, etc.) and $100 in revenue, making $40 in profit. If a copycat took 50% of your market, each of you would make $50 in revenue. As costs would still be of $60 for both of you, because they're fixed, then both of you would lose $10 each. In this situation, the competitor would be deterred because there is no more room for another profitable company in the market. Economist Bruce Greenwald explains:

> Consider the case of an isolated town in Nebraska with a population of fifty thousand or less. A town of this size can support only one large discount store. A determined retailer who develops such a store should expect to enjoy an unchallenged monopoly. If a second store were

to enter the town, neither would have enough customer traffic to be profitable. Other things being equal, the second entrant could not expect to drive out the first, so its best choice would be to stay away, leaving the monopoly intact.[36]

This type of "natural monopoly" occurs when fixed costs are high (think of a sophisticated product) compared to the market size (think of a specialized, niche product). This may be the golden nugget so many entrepreneurs are looking for!

I met an entrepreneur who built a software start-up that helps aerospace companies coordinate their logistics. The start-up is highly profitable and the return on investment has been enormous. Copycats are unlikely to be interested in copying it because it's protected by the small-scale moat—the product is non-trivial, and thus costly to build, and it targets a niche domain, so the market is small. Because businesses like this one don't promise billion-dollar revenue, they're often overlooked by entrepreneurs and investors. But bigger is not always better.

### *The Brand Illusion*

The word "Google" has turned into a verb; it has even been added to most major dictionaries like Oxford and Webster's. The strength of Google's brand is undeniable. However, this hasn't been cheap to maintain. In 2023, it was revealed that Google had been paying billions to Apple, Samsung, and other smartphone manufacturers in order to remain the default search engine in their web browsers. In 2021 alone, Google spent $23.6 billion for that privilege.[37] This sum represented a whopping 29% of Google's profits from ads.[38] The word "Google" may have made its way to the dictionary, but this has come at a high cost.

Many books on business strategy cite branding as a type of moat. They argue that by making your name widely known and associated with positive emotions, you can hold customers captive. Back in 2019, an online entrepreneur argued, "WeWork's very name is now a well-known byword for the service it offers. A lot of the uninitiated have no idea how many other options they have. They just hear co-working and translate that to WeWork. The perception advantage that it has is massive."[39]

In reality, the fact that brands can be true moats has been disputed. This is because they are often surprisingly expensive to maintain, as the Google example illustrates, and opportunities to promote a brand are often available to higher-bidding competitors. Bruce Greenwald explains, "The Mercedes Benz brand does not maintain itself; it needs to be replenished with fresh advertising and image-burnishing expenses. … Despite the many years that Mercedes has spent investing in the brand, there is nothing to keep competing car companies from following its lead."[40] Greenwald adds that Mercedes has not provided great returns to investors despite its status as a premium brand.

Business strategist Hamilton Helmers thinks brands can be powerful moats but only after decades of building a positive reputation. He says, "A strong brand can only be created over a lengthy period of reinforced actions" and cites the example of Tiffany's, which "cultivated its brand name for more than a century."[41] Start-ups don't usually have that much time.

Some people argue that having a well-known name can

become a moat but only with cheap products for which people don't bother researching alternatives. Greenwald argues, "For a company to take a substantial market share from WD-40, it would need not only to spend a fortune on advertising and distribution but also to price its products at a significant discount to WD-40. WD-40's products are small-ticket items, bought infrequently by consumers but with great loyalty. ... A competitive product priced at 10 percent less would hardly entice customers away from a brand they know and trust for a savings of 30 cents."[42]

In the digital world, this makes me think of Canva, the browser-based design tool for simple social media graphics. The tool filled a market gap, so it grew fast (profitably) and soon became well known. As it provides many useful features for free, and its premium version is cheap, I've noticed that many people gravitate toward Canva by default without researching alternatives. But when stakes are higher, as in the case of buying a WeWork subscription, customers are much less loyal, so most start-ups cannot just spend a fortune to grow fast and hope that having well-known names will protect them from competitors.

## GROWTH: AN OBSESSION

Every time we hear about a start-up growing fast, perhaps we should ask ourselves *why* it has to grow fast. That question doesn't seem to be asked often enough. Part of the obsession with growth is that start-ups want to protect themselves from copycats. But perhaps *they* are the copycats! They try to grow fast to copy what Facebook or Amazon did, thinking they'll obtain the same results. They forget they need to build a moat for expensive growth to be worth it, or they underestimate how hard it is to build one.

The obsessive focus on growth has made many entrepreneurs think that obtaining money from venture capitalists is always necessary to succeed. So, for them, raising money has become a major goal in and of itself. I've met many entrepreneurs who raised money without knowing what they'd use it for. One of them tried to raise a first million dollars as fast as he could just because the seven-figure number would look good and help attract more funding.

An investor provided the following advice on LinkedIn: "Raising $500k is harder than raising $1 million. Why? Because it makes an investor think you lack ambition. You actually limit an investor's belief that you will be successful if you decide to raise less money." A former venture capitalist told me he thinks many entrepreneurs raise funding as a rite of passage or to get a seal of approval.

Raising money has also become a common yardstick to measure a start-up's success. In networking events, I often hear phrases such as, "That start-up is doing really well. It just raised twenty million!" However, a company truly does well when it finds a way to make sustained profits. That's how it pays the bills in the long run.

But paying the bills is usually not such a big problem for many start-ups, as they keep receiving money from others to cover their losses. Let's follow the money trail to see where those funds come from. This leads us to venture capital.

# CHAPTER 3

# VENTURE CAPITAL

Venture capitalists are facilitators of innovation—by making bold investments, they support ambitious entrepreneurs who want to change the world. Notably, venture capitalists provided early funding to Apple, Amazon, Facebook, Google, and Microsoft. A Forbes article explains, "This category of investment and funding keeps the economy from stagnating. VC is an important engine of economic growth and progress, both in the U.S. and around the globe."[1] The article suggests that venture capital works well both for entrepreneurs and investors: "For entrepreneurs, VC capital and support represent a lifeline. … For investors, VC provides a chance to put their money into innovative companies with growth potential."

Other people don't see it that way. For example, billionaire businessman Charlie Munger used to be very vocal about his skepticism of venture capital. He once said, "You don't want to make money by screwing your investors and that's what a lot of venture capitalists do."[2] Such negative sentiment around venture capital seems to be taking hold as of late, especially as the industry doesn't seem to be providing great returns to its investors. Two notorious scandals have also fueled the negative sentiment. One was Theranos, a start-up which developed a blood-testing device that didn't work as intended and covered it up for years, while receiving hundreds of millions of VC money. The other was FTX, a cryptocurrency trading app which secretly diverted its clients' funds into another company, while also receiving hundreds of millions from VCs. The founders of both start-ups were convicted of fraud.

In this chapter, we discuss the world of venture capital. We first describe how the industry works, what it promises, and what it delivers. We then discuss whether a more cynical account, such as the one espoused by Charlie Munger, is consistent with the evidence.

## HOW VENTURE CAPITAL WORKS

A venture capital firm is an investment management company that decides how to invest other people's money—and some of its own—into start-ups. The first job of a VC firm is to raise money from others, such as pension funds and wealthy individuals. The VC firm creates a separate legal entity, known as a *fund*, which is responsible for the pot of money raised. The fund has a limited duration (usually ten years) and a fixed size—no more money can be added into it after the initial fundraising. The typical size of a fund is $100 million, although in recent years there's been a rise of mega-funds, which can go above one billion. The VC firm usually puts some of its own money into the fund—around 1% of it—to have more skin in the game.

The fund is wholly managed by the VC firm, which decides

how to allocate the money. The outsiders who provide most of the fund's money are known as limited partners, or LPs, because they put money into the fund but do not decide how it is used.

Over the first five years of a fund, the VC firm chooses which start-ups to invest the fund's money in. For that, the VC goes through the painstaking process of interviewing hundreds of candidates and sifting through never-ending PowerPoint presentations known as *pitch decks,* which entrepreneurs use to promote their business ideas. The VC firm usually hires junior associates to do much of the legwork of filtering start-ups before leaving important investment decisions to senior managers.

When the VC identifies a promising start-up, it makes an offer to buy a portion of it from the founders or current owners. For example, a VC may offer to buy 10% of a start-up in exchange for $10 million. If the deal goes through, the start-up receives a useful injection of cash, which can be used to grow the business, at the expense of giving up 10% of its ownership.

When a VC makes an offer, it must carefully decide how much the start-up is worth, known as its *valuation.* For example, if a VC offers to buy 10% of a start-up for $10 million, it considers the total value of the start-up to be $100 million. If the deal goes through, the start-up is said to be valued at $100 million. If a VC pays, say, $100 million for 10% of a start-up, it gives the start-up a valuation of one billion dollars, turning it into a unicorn. Note that a start-up's valuation—unicorn or not—represents how enthusiastic the VC was when purchasing a portion of it, and the figure is not directly tied to a fundamental business metric like profit or sales.

Every year, in exchange for the service of selecting and striking deals with start-ups, the VC firm charges the LPs a management fee of 2% of the invested capital. From a fully invested $100-million fund, for example, the VC charges $2 million a year in management fees to the LPs. The LPs must also reimburse some of the VC's expenses, such as travel and accommodation to attend board meetings. The management fee is charged independently of the success of the fund's investments. Even if all of the start-ups in the fund failed and thus LPs lost all their invested money, the VC firm would still collect the management fee. We shall return to this point later.

During the first five years of a fund, the VC must select all the start-ups it wants to invest the fund's money in, usually ten or more. After the five-year anniversary of the fund, the VC is not allowed to pick any new start-ups. However, if there's any leftover money, the VC firm can invest it in the start-ups already selected. After year five, the VC firm starts charging the LPs a lower management fee of 1% of the fund's invested money per year.

Once investments have been made, the VC holds them for a few years and then tries to *exit* them, meaning that it tries to sell its shares to others in exchange for cash. The VC firm hopes to make a profit by selling the shares for more money than it bought them for. Usually, the VC distributes the proceeds immediately to the LPs after each exit. However, the VC firm takes a 20% cut of the profits, called the *carry*, before transferring the remaining 80% to the LPs. This is why the VC compensation structure is often known as "2 and 20," which means 2% in yearly management fees and a 20% cut of profits. By year ten, the VC is expected to exit all of the fund's investments.

There are three main types of exits. The most common one happens when a start-up is bought, or *acquired*, by a larger company. For example, Instagram was bought by Facebook for $1 billion. The proceeds from an acquisition are distributed to VC funds proportionally to their percentage ownership. If a fund owns, say, 10% of a start-up sold for $100 million, it obtains $10 million. Or at least that's the case when the acquisition is satisfactory.

If things don't go so well, more often than not, the arrangement between start-up founders and VCs grants the latter a sort of "money-back guarantee." So, if the sale of the start-up isn't good enough to return to the VC the money it originally invested, then the founders must use their own proceeds from the sale to pay them their money back. This can leave the founders empty-handed. This is a reality that VC-backed entrepreneurs must always be prepared for: Despite years of effort and a multi-million-dollar sale, they may walk out with little or no money at all.

This money-back guarantee attributes a dual role to the VC fund: it acts as a partner or a lender depending on the circumstances. In favorable circumstances, the VC acts like a partner because it reaps a reward proportional to its ownership in the company. In unfavorable circumstances, the VC acts like a lender because it requests as much of its money back as possible before anybody else is paid. VCs certainly love to have their cake and eat it too! VCs also tend to get veto rights over important decisions, such as accepting acquisition offers.

The second most common type of exit takes place in the event of an initial public offering, or *IPO,* which is when a start-up sells its shares for the first time in a public market, such as the New York Stock Exchange. During the IPO or sometime later, VCs can exit their positions by selling their shares in the open market in exchange for cash. VCs sometimes have a "money-back guarantee" to protect them in the case of an unfavorable IPO.[3]

The third way for a VC to exit its investment is to sell its shares privately to a third party, perhaps another fund. This is known as a *secondary sale*. VCs tend to prefer an acquisition or an IPO, but they may choose to sell their shares in the secondary market early on if the opportunity seems right.

If a fund's life is coming to an end but it still hasn't exited all its investments, the VC manager may choose to extend the fund's lifetime by another two years. After that, the LPs vote every year on whether to extend the fund by another year or not. If not, the VC may have no choice but to sell the remaining shares immediately in the secondary market or transfer them to the LPs. In practice, the average fund gets extended to fifteen years.[4]

Venture capital is risky, so one may think regulation would limit who can invest in it. For example, one may think pension funds, which are tightly regulated, wouldn't be allowed to invest employees' life savings in venture capital. However, while such regulation exists, it's often very easy to get around. For example, in the U.S., pension funds are allowed to invest in venture capital provided that the VC fund can have some influence in the management of the start-ups it invests in—and it turns out this requirement is satisfied very easily. When a VC fund invests in a start-up, it usually requests the right to appoint a member to its board of directors, and this is enough to say it has some control over the start-up and thus waive regulatory impediments. A lawyer explains that the path to let pension funds invest in venture capital "is generally pretty clear and potentially self-executing for many venture capital funds."[5]

## THE PROMISE

Venture capitalists promise LPs a large return on investment compared to alternatives, such as buying a portfolio of stocks in the public market. As a rule of thumb, LPs expect—and are promised—to multiply their money by at least 2.5 times, which is often described as a "2.5x return,"[6] while holding each start-up investment for around five years before exiting it. For comparison, the stock market has historically generated a 1.6x return in a five-year period.[7]

The LPs expect a higher return compared to the stock market for two reasons. First, their money is locked in for a few years, compared to holding public stocks, which can be easily sold off at any time, so they expect to be compensated for that restriction. Second, investment in start-ups has a larger downside compared to other forms of investment—a lot of start-ups lose all of their investors' money. LPs expect a higher return as compensation for their risk-taking.

Venture capitalists claim to have found a winning formula that can multiply LPs' money by 2.5x or more. The formula exploits the *skewness* of investing in risky start-ups. The rationale is as follows: While a large proportion of start-ups fail, a minority of them win really big, which ends up far outweighing the losses. VCs call this the *power law*—a mathematical term used to describe highly skewed random events.

When VCs describe their strategy, especially when investing in early-stage start-ups, they often cite the *rule of thirds:* "We expect to lose our entire investment on one third of our investments, we expect to get our money back (or maybe make a small return) on one third of our investments, and we expect to generate the bulk of our returns on one third of our investments."[8]

Under the rule of thirds, the winning start-ups in the portfolio must return an average of at least 9x in order to compensate for the subpar performance of the rest and return the desired 2.5x to LPs:

|  | Losers | OK | Big winners |
| --- | --- | --- | --- |
| Proportion | ⅓ | ⅓ | ⅓ |
| Return | 0x | 1x | 9x |

Total return: 3.33x
Minus 20% (VC firm's cut)
Minus management fees

Return to LPs: 2.5x

The success of this strategy hinges on how realistic its assumptions are. If, for example, VCs aren't able to generate an average of 9x return from the third of winning start-ups, then the strategy won't work. The same can be said if start-ups fail more often than suggested by the rule of thirds.

There's a common narrative that claims that VCs *must* pick start-ups with the potential to make a significant return, higher than 9x, because, as too many start-ups fail, winners must win big to make up for the losses. As a result, VCs must only make bold investments into ambitious start-ups. An investor explains that if VCs reject your start-up idea because it's not big enough, "it just means that VCs need to shoot for sky-high multiples to make up for their investments that don't work."[9]

A Forbes article encourages entrepreneurs to focus on large markets because "a VC firm needs a few deals to generate substantial returns, so as to offset the inevitable losers."[10] In a similar direction, entrepreneur Peter Thiel explains, "The biggest secret in venture capital is that the best investment in a successful fund equals or outperforms the entire rest of the fund combined. This implies a strange rule for VCs: only invest in companies that have the potential to return the value of the entire fund. This is a scary rule, because it eliminates the vast majority of possible investments."[11]

This narrative considers the power law to be the cause of bold investments:

Power law → Bold investments

Under this view, the power law just happens, inevitably. So, VCs have no choice but to make bold investments to make up for the all-too-common poor outcomes. In reality, it's the exact other way around:

Bold investments → Power law

It is the boldness of VCs' investments that causes the power law. By investing in miracle-hoping start-ups like WeWork, VCs observe highly skewed, power-law returns. This is because miracles don't happen often, so a majority of the start-ups produce meager returns or even lose all of their investors' money. However, when a miracle does happen, it comes as such as surprise that it generates impressive returns. An investment analyst explained, "VC funds invest in a particular type of startup, one that is much more likely to go to zero, but which has the potential, if it does succeed, to produce something very big."[12] So, bold investments simultaneously reduce the chances of success and increase the payout in the case of success. The result is the power law. VCs hope that victories will outweigh defeats and thus produce high returns overall:

Bold investments → Power law → High returns (hope)

Let's see how this has been playing out.

## THE RESULTS

VC firms rarely disclose performance figures to the public, and their LPs are contractually forbidden from doing so. Sequoia Capital, the world's second largest VC firm, went as far as cutting its twenty-two-year relationship with an LP for fear that a Freedom of Information Act request would force it to share performance figures publicly.[13]

But not all is lost. Over the past two decades, at least a couple of organizations have collected and tracked performance data of hundreds of VC funds, without naming names. One of them is an investment consulting company called Cambridge Associates. In a 2020 report, it shared the performance of 1,529 VC funds launched since 1995.[14] Performance data was shared voluntarily to them over the years by fund managers. Another similar report was published in 2020 by the U.S. National Bureau of Economic Research (NBER), which shared performance metrics of 1,329 VC funds launched between 1984 and 2014.[15] In this case, the data was sourced from an analytics company that many LPs rely on for record-keeping. Here are the results:

## Average VC Fund Return by Launch Year

*Legend: Cambridge Associates — NBER — 2.5x*

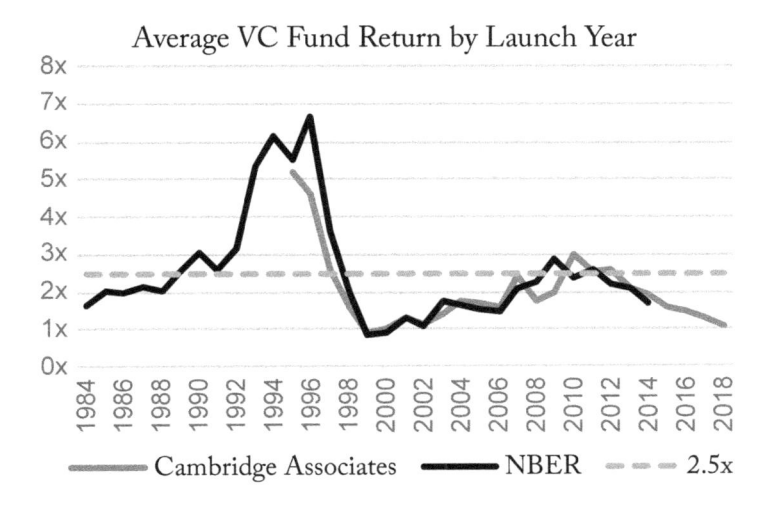

We can see that, on average, only VC funds launched right before the height of the dot-com bubble generated impressive returns (mostly by selling their shares to the public for inflated prices before the crash). Since then, however, VC performance has been underwhelming at best; in fact, most of the time VC has *not* generated the promised 2.5x return to LPs.

As the promised 2.5x return isn't attained most of the time, then the rule of thirds must be overly optimistic. The evidence suggest that this is indeed the case. For example, the European Investment Fund analyzed the returns generated by 2,065 individual VC exits from start-up investments.[16] Successful exits generated an average return of around 4x, much less than the required 9x according to the rule of thirds. Moreover, only 29% of exits generated a profit for investors or paid them their money back, against the expected 66% according to the rule of thirds. The data also showed that a whopping 57% of start-ups lost all of VCs' money or returned a symbolic 0.25x upon liquidation. Data from U.S. exits also suggests that the rule of thirds is overly optimistic. A study of twenty-seven thousand U.S. exits in the 2009–2018 period showed that 64% incurred a loss for VCs.[17] The study was later repeated on over thirty-five thousand U.S. exits in the period 2013–2022, and the data showed that 48% of them were money-losing for VCs.[18]

As the numbers suggest, the winners under the power law don't seem to offset the losers as much as expected. Entrepreneur Karam Hinduja called the strategy "spray and pray" and suggested that VC funds "invest in 60 companies and hope that one or two turn out to be the next unicorn. There is too little focus on identifying and nurturing the robust, financially dependable businesses that should be at the heart of a stable economy."[19] Entrepreneur and venture capitalist Fredrick D. Scott said the same thing less nicely: "When you really boil this 'investing' style down to simpler terms, it's really just throwing sh*t against a wall in the hopes that something will stick."[20]

As VCs don't generate good returns overall, it has become customary to highlight that the top VC funds *do* generate good returns. In particular, industry promoters tend to share performance figures of the top 25% of VCs, or the *top quartile*. The founder of a VC firm explained, "Top quartile VC funds generate strong returns," and "The top one percentile, meaning those that generate better returns than 99% of their peers, generate outstanding returns."[21]

A study of 1,329 funds showed that, indeed, funds in the top 25% generated returns that exceeded, on average, the desired 2.5x, although not as much since the dot-com crash. The other three quartiles, covering the bottom 75% of funds, did not provide good returns on average:[22]

| Ranking | Average return | |
|---|---|---|
| Top 25% | 5.34x | 3.84x |
| 25%–50% | 2.16x | 1.85x |
| 50%–75% | 1.32x | 1.30x |
| Bottom 25% | 0.69x | 0.72x |
| | Funds launched up to 2000 | Funds launched since 2001 |

This kind of analysis is problematic because the observation that top funds perform better than the rest is self-fulfilling. Similarly, if you measured the height of the top 25% tallest people in a city, then they'd be rather tall on average! It is tempting to think that there's a group of talented VC firms at the top whose strategy is superior. However, it could be out of pure randomness or luck that the top funds end up at the top.

If the different funds managed by the same VC firm were consistently at the top, then we could argue that their investment strategy is superior. A study showed that there is a little bit of persistence in the firms whose funds end up at the top. Such persistence is, however, quite mild and cannot be successfully exploited by LPs. Suppose a firm with a fund currently in the top 25% raises another fund. The new fund has a 33% chance of ending up in the top 25%.[23] This is a bit higher than random, which would only give the new fund a 25% chance of being in the top 25%, but there is still a whopping 67% chance of the fund landing in the underperforming 75%.

Moreover, a study suggested that the mild persistence of top firms may not really be down to talent. Instead, an initially good strike, due to luck, makes the VC firm more prestigious and gives it access to better deals: "Entrepreneurs accept lower valuations and less attractive terms from more prestigious VC firms when choosing between offers."[24] In addition, the persistence of funds at the top fades over time: "VC firms with larger numbers of investments converge to the industry average success rate."

These results suggest that the VC model does not work well for LPs in general. Only a lucky few make good money, and it's unlikely that they can repeat that in the next fund. The portion of your pension money or university tuition funneled to VCs will likely not be multiplied as much as promised and not in a way that justifies the risk taken. However, as we'll see next, although the VC model may not be working well for others, it may be working well for the VCs themselves.

## MANAGEMENT FEES

Imagine that a real estate agency charged you a management fee just for listing your property, regardless of them selling it. You might worry the agency won't work hard enough to sell your property, as it will collect a fee regardless. You might even worry the agency will just focus on finding more properties to list, in order to collect more fees, rather than on selling yours. That's why most real-estate agencies operate on a "no sale, no fee" basis.

Unlike real estate agencies, venture capital firms make money regardless of their results. Over the life of a ten-year fund, the VC firm collects a total of around 15% of the fund's size in management fees, at a rate of 2% a year during the first five years and 1% afterward. From a typical $100-million fund, for example, the VC firm collects $15 million in management fees.

A great way for VC firms to make more money is to raise a new, separate fund quickly after the previous one—and that's exactly what they do. On average, VC firms raise a new fund every 2.25 years.[25] This has led to the rise of mega-VC firms. Andreessen Horowitz, currently the world's largest VC firm, raised a multitude of funds for a total of $35 billion during a seven-year period. In just one year, the record-breaking 2021, it raised "a $4.5 billion crypto fund, a $5 billion growth fund, a $2.5 billion venture fund, and a $1.5 billion bio fund."[26] The firm collects half a billion dollars a year just from management fees. Sequoia Capital, the second-largest VC firm, has raised $26 billion across several funds in the period 2018–2022[27] and also collects hundreds of millions in management fees every year.

The administrative costs of running each extra fund aren't too high for the VC firm, so much of the additional management fees translate into profits. Venture capitalist Brad Feld explains, "Although venture capital firms tend to grow head count as they raise new funds, this isn't always the case and the head count rarely grows in direct proportion to the increased management fees. As a result, the senior partners of the venture capital firm see their base compensation rise with each additional fund."[28]

Receiving such high compensation independently of results has made a lot of people doubtful of VCs' incentives. Charlie Munger explained:

> Back in 2000, venture-capital funds raised $100 billion and put it into Internet startups—$100 billion! They would have been better off taking at least $50 billion of it, putting it into bushel baskets and lighting it on fire

with an acetylene torch. That's the kind of madness you get with fee-driven investment management. Everyone wants to be an investment manager, raise the maximum amount of money, trade like mad with one another, and then just scrape the fees off the top. I know one guy, he's extremely smart and a very capable investor. I asked him, 'What returns do you tell your institutional clients you will earn for them?' He said, '20%.' I couldn't believe it, because he knows that's impossible. But he said, 'Charlie, if I gave them a lower number, they wouldn't give me any money to invest!' The investment management business is insane.[29]

A disappointed LP published a report saying that when you give money to VCs, "you get what you pay for," suggesting that VCs are paid well "to build funds, not build companies." The report explains:

> The most significant misalignment occurs because LPs don't pay VCs to do what they say they will—generate returns that exceed the public market. Instead, VCs typically are paid a 2 percent management fee on committed capital and a 20 percent profit-sharing structure (known as "2 and 20"). This pays VCs more for raising bigger funds, and in many cases allows them to lock in high levels of fee-based personal income even when the general partner fails to return investor capital.[30]

In 2022, a *Fortune* article explained that critics "accuse Andreessen Horowitz of *stacking fees,* or raising so much money that it can profit off management fees alone without relying on carry—or its cut of the actual performance of its investments. As the firm expands into different areas of the financial markets, its growing catalog of assets should generate ever more management fees."[31]

If VCs generated good results overall, it would be hard to believe they'd be highly motivated by management fees, as the 20% cut on profits from successful investments could be much higher. However, as we saw above, the performance of VC funds isn't that great overall, so management fees are a sizable portion of VC firms' income. Professor of Law Katherine Litvak studied sixty-eight venture capital funds and found out that "about half of total VC compensation comes from the non-risky management fee." She concluded, "VC compensation is less performance-based than commonly believed."[32] Even the founder of a venture capital firm admitted, "Most funds never return enough profit for their managers to see a dime of the 20% carried interest. Instead, the management fees are how they get paid."[33]

One would think that, in the long run, focusing on management fees and underdelivering to the LPs would be career-ending for a VC manager. However, some people have argued the contrary: because LPs "rely on relationships when making investment decisions,"[34] they're likely to continue working with managers they know even if their past results weren't great.

As we'll see next, high management fees have made some people believe that VCs use questionable tactics to raise more and more funds.

## A PONZI SCHEME?

In 2012, the Kauffman Foundation, an American non-profit organization, decided to analyze its past twenty years of investing in VC funds as an LP. The foundation published a worrying result: The VC funds in which they invested tended to report to them an exceedingly high performance during the first two years. That coincided with the period during which their managers were trying to raise a new fund. After the first two years passed, the reported performance dropped dramatically and remained low:

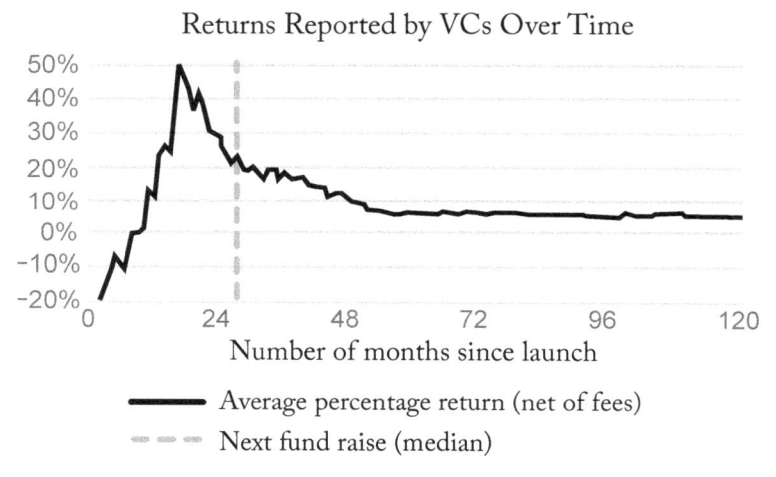

### Returns Reported by VCs Over Time

*(Chart: Y-axis from -20% to 50%; X-axis "Number of months since launch" from 0 to 120. Average percentage return (net of fees) peaks near ~50% around month 18–20, then declines sharply and levels off near 5%. Dashed vertical line indicates Next fund raise (median) around month 24.)*

— Average percentage return (net of fees)
- - - Next fund raise (median)

The foundation concluded that fund managers either manipulated their early return figures or only worked hard during the first few months of a fund, which let them promote good figures to others when trying to raise the next fund. The foundation stated, "Distressingly, fund managers focus on the front end of a fund's performance period because that performance drives a successful fundraising outcome in subsequent funds." Their report also suggested that VCs "write up portfolio company valuations considerably and frequently early in their fund's life, which results in positive returns" and then performance "retreats precipitously over the remaining term of fund life." The foundation explained that this tendency became more pronounced after 1995: "Our best-performing funds—those launched prior to 1995—did not report peak returns until the sixth or the seventh year of their lives. That pattern began to change in the late '90s, when peak returns almost always were reported during the fund's five-year investment period, usually in the first thirty-six months."

In 2016, a systematic study of 1,074 funds tried to ascertain whether fund managers tried to manipulate their reported returns. The evidence showed that, indeed, at the time of raising their next funds "under-performing fund managers boosted reported returns." After that, the reported performance dropped sharply.[35] The study showed, however, that overstating performance is counterproductive if overdone, as LPs "see through much of the manipulation." The authors suggested the spike in early reported returns may not necessarily be due to intentional manipulation. For example, it could be that after the new fund is raised, VCs "dedicate most of their efforts (and possibly better deals) to the new fund." Even if that's the case, the article argues that it still represents a "cost born by LPs in the old fund."

To understand how this is even possible, let's see how VCs calculate their returns. Early on in the life of a fund, most of the investments haven't been exited yet. So, the VC calculates an estimation of future, or *unrealized,* gains that it expects to make later on. VCs use different methods to calculate such unrealized gains, and they are all somehow subjective. The VC firm Andreessen Horowitz explains on its website that performing such calculation is "more of an art than a science" and that, to some extent, the resulting figure is "in the eye of the beholder."[36]

One method to calculate unrealized gains, for example, is

to estimate the increase in value of a start-up by comparing it with similar companies that trade in public markets. Andreesen Horowitz explains, "If a portfolio company is generating $100 million of revenue and its 'comparable' set of companies are valued in the public markets at 5x revenue, a venture firm would then value the company at $500 million."

Another method to calculate unrealized gains, probably the most common one today, is to compare the original valuation given by the VC against the valuation given by VCs in the latest investment round. Suppose the first VC invests in a start-up at a valuation of $10 million, and then another VC invests in the same start-up at a valuation of $15 million. The first VC counts that as a 1.5x unrealized gain. The calculation is still somehow subjective as it depends on another VC's perceived valuation of the start-up—if the latter VC gives the start-up an excessively high valuation, the former VC reports an impressive unrealized gain. Note that raising money for a lower valuation than in a previous round causes an unrealized loss for early investors, so it's a rare and dreaded event.[37]

This has led some people to believe that VCs continuously try to jack up valuations in order to inflate unrealized gains. In a critical open letter, a venture capitalist explained:

> VCs habitually invest in one another's companies during later rounds, bidding up rounds to valuations that allow for generous markups on their funds' performance. These markups, and the paper returns that they suggest, allow VCs to raise subsequent, larger funds, and to enjoy the management fees that those funds generate. … Even if paying or marking up sky-high valuations will make it less likely that a fund manager will ever see their

share of earned profit, it makes it more likely they'll get to raise larger funds—and earn enormous management fees. There's some deep misalignment here.[38]

The author then concludes, "The dynamics we've entered is, in many ways, creating a dangerous, high-stakes Ponzi scheme." A Ponzi scheme is a type of fraud in which a con artist generates fake or unsustainable gains for early investors and promotes those gains to lure more and more investors.

Some people have also suggested that the metrics VCs use to report their performance are sometimes misunderstood or even manipulated. A popular metric used is the internal rate of return, or *IRR*. This metric converts the return multiple, including unrealized returns, into a yearly percentage, say, from "2.5x" into "30% per year." The metric became popular because investors are used to speaking in terms of yearly percentage returns when analyzing investments in public markets like stocks or bonds.

The IRR is calculated in a convoluted way that seeks to reward early returns over later returns. So, if a fund exits some of its investments earlier than others, this pushes the percentage value upwards.[39] The metric has been criticized on two fronts. First, some people say it's prone to manipulation or short-sightedness. The Kauffman Foundation, for example, argues that VCs are encouraged to generate "short-term, high IRRs by 'flipping' companies rather than committing to long-term, scale growth of a start-up."[40] Second, the IRR figure is often compared side-by-side with percentage returns from the stock market, but this is misleading because the two are calculated differently (with the IRR figure being pushed upward compared to an ordinary return in the event of an early exit).

Economist Ludovic Phalippou explains, "If the IRR is being thought of as a rate of return that an investor actually earns, it is implausibly high. When an implausibly high IRR of this sort is presented as if it was a rate of return that is comparable to stock-market rates of return, I believe that is unquestionably misleading."[41] According to Phalippou, the IRR is too often compared directly with stock market returns. However, rather than this being due to intentional manipulation, he argues that a lot of people "do not seem to understand what the key flaw of IRR is."

## THE GREATER FOOL?

In July 2019, it was revealed that Adam Neumann, the founder of WeWork, had been cashing out on his WeWork shares privately. He had sold a portion of his shares to others and used the rest to secure loans from banks. In total, he collected $700 million in cash from those deals. A few months later, in September 2019, WeWork had to infamously cancel its initial public offering, and enthusiasm about the company collapsed beyond repair. Adam Neumann cashed out at the right time.

In order to make money from selling shares of a start-up, an enthusiastic buyer must be willing to pay good money for them. This is possible if the company exhibits genuinely strong prospects. However, some people argue that it's also possible to make money from an overvalued start-up despite its lack of genuine value; all it takes is to find a buyer willing to overpay even more. Perhaps that same buyer will make a profit by selling their shares to someone willing to overpay even more, and so on. The key is to cash out early enough, before the house of cards collapses. This is informally known as the greater fool theory. Economics professor Vicki Bogan explains:

> The Greater Fool Theory is the idea that, during a market bubble, one can make money by buying overvalued assets and selling them for a profit later, because it will always be possible to find someone who is willing to pay a higher price. ... Unfortunately, when the bubble eventually bursts (which it always does), you can lose a great deal of money if you are the one left holding the asset and cannot find a buyer.[42]

There is a growing sentiment that the greater fool theory applies to the world of start-ups. In a critical analysis of the VC industry, investment banker Karam Hinduja explains, "Venture capitalists get on board at valuation X, and then attempt to jack up the perceived value of the company to X+10 for the next investor so that the early investors can make a return."[43] In an equally critical analysis, billionaire entrepreneur Narayana Murthy explains, "I am in series B. I sell my first deal at a profit, I get off and it is the series Z fellow that is left with the tin box,"[44] where "series A," "series B," and so on, are usually used to denote the successive rounds of funding received by a start-up.

A tech entrepreneur also laments the status of venture capital, arguing that it is "dominated by a closed circle of VCs who share deal flow amongst themselves and fund their investment progenies with sky high valuations, knowing that their initial involvement will lead to even higher valuations when more investors are lured into the deal. On Wall Street this investment approach is known as The Greater Fool Theory."[45]

The greater fool theory, if true, could be well aligned with the interests of many of the people involved in a start-up, including VCs, LPs, founders, and CEOs, as they can all benefit from selling shares at the height of a bubble. Karam Hinduja explains, "The founders and CEOs of the companies play into this. Instead of building sound businesses, they focus on 'positioning' their companies for the next funding round—effectively playing branding and marketing roles in order to court the next group of investors or to get bought by a bigger firm, instead of properly managing their revenues, costs, and operations." Indeed, as we saw earlier, Adam Neumann made a lot of money thanks to the excessively high expectations about WeWork, before enthusiasm waned. We also saw that VC investments generated impressive returns in the late 1990's by riding the dot-com bubble and cashing out before it burst.

If there is some truth to the greater fool theory, then it must require some outstanding storytelling skills to convince others to jump on the boat.

## TELLING GOOD STORIES

In 2019, trader Sam Bankman-Fried launched a start-up called FTX, which let users invest in cryptocurrencies. Two years later, the start-up raised $900 million from various VC firms. One of them was Sequoia Capital, which handed FTX a check for $214 million. Sequoia published a dramatic biography of Sam Bankman-Fried on its website, describing his career and life choices. The biography contained thirteen thousand words, which is approximately two chapters of this book and longer than Wikipedia's article on Queen Elizabeth II. The biography started by describing Bankman's earlier career achievements and charitable activities. For example, it mentioned that he used to give away "50 percent of his income to his preferred charities" and that "he had a personal blog where he wrote about his search for life's meaning."[46]

The biography then moved on to Bankman's impressive hard work: "Sam Bankman-Fried just keeps working and working. He's working when people arrive. He's working when people leave. It's Zoom after Zoom after Zoom, and, because Sam Bankman-Fried wears a headset, he's literally plugged into his computer all day. The only time I ever see him unplug is to collapse on that supersized beanbag chair next to his desk for a catnap." The article then showed a picture of Sam Bankman-Fried taking a nap in his office on a large beanbag. Sequoia removed the biography when it was revealed that FTX was committing widespread fraud.

As we can see from the epic biography of Sam Bankman-Fried, venture capitalists are masters of storytelling. They also love to work with founders with great storytelling skills. Historian Margaret O'Mara explained, "Being able to tell a good story is part of being a successful founder, being able to persuade investors to put money into your company."[47] This even applies to PowerPoint presentations. A venture capitalist explained that when looking at a founder's presentation slides, "Investors are not solely evaluating your company's story. They are also evaluating your ability to convey that story."[48]

Adam Neumann, the founder of WeWork, was well known for his outstanding storytelling skills. In 2015, a set of fundraising documents were leaked which revealed how Neumann had presented WeWork to VCs in order to raise $355 million. A technology reporter thoroughly analyzed the documents and concluded:

The story is a good one. All told, the fundraising documents portray a company on a phenomenal trajectory. Profits, membership, and locations grow at an enviable rate, while occupancy hovers just below 100%. But the material also reveals that WeWork relied on enormous demand projections and certain accounting tricks—both of which are popular tactics among private companies—to keep its profit margins looking as high as its aspirations. ... WeWork has mastered the kind of storytelling that locks down massive rounds and can earn what is essentially a real estate company the privilege of being discussed as—and valued like—a nimble Silicon Valley software startup.[49]

You would think Neumann would struggle to receive support from VCs later on, after he was widely criticized for his handling of WeWork and removed from the company. But that wasn't the case. Three years after leaving WeWork, Neumann launched a new real estate start-up called Flow. The VC firm Andreessen Horowitz invested a whopping $350 million in the start-up. This turned Flow into a unicorn automatically, before it even opened its doors. It was Andreessen Horowitz's largest check ever.[50]

Neumann's new company will tackle the area of private housing, but it is unclear exactly how. Andreessen Horowitz suggested the company will combine "community-driven, experience-centric service with the latest technology in a way that has never been done before to create a system where renters receive the benefits of owners."[51] The VC firm also explained that Flow's theme will be "connecting people through transforming their physical spaces and building communities where people spend the most time: their homes." It's hard to figure this out, but the cryptic wording is strikingly similar to that of WeWork.

Andreessen Horowitz explained its decision:

> Adam is a visionary leader who revolutionized the second largest asset class in the world—commercial real estate—by bringing community and brand to an industry in which neither existed before. ... It's often underappreciated that only one person has fundamentally redesigned the office experience and led a paradigm-changing global company in the process: Adam Neumann. We understand how difficult it is to build something like this and we love seeing repeat-founders build on past successes by growing from lessons learned.

Perhaps Andreessen Horowitz supported Neumann because an energetic founder with great communication skills is great for business. But, if we believe in the greater fool theory, there's an alternative, cynical explanation. Perhaps the VC firm chose to work with a founder with great storytelling skills because it wanted him to tell good stories to the next round of investors.

Those who subscribe to the greater fool theory have also pointed out that storytelling may be behind VCs' never-ending enthusiasm for the "next big thing," such as blockchain, generative AI, NFTs and self-driving cars. Maybe they genuinely believe in the transformational power of these technologies. Or, perhaps, they like how big they sound and the great stories they tell. Entrepreneur Karam Hinduja suggested that VC firms have become "an echo chamber, one fueling the other with claims that they have found the next big thing. ... Robotics or artificial intelligence may certainly make great headlines, but sound financial models too rarely factor into the equation."[52] A technology reporter even argued that the early hype around ChatGPT was an attempt by VCs to divert attention from the slump experienced by the tech sector in 2022: "Silicon Valley is hoping and praying that AI hype can keep customers and investors distracted until their balance sheets can bounce back."[53]

The tech sector may be the perfect breeding ground for exaggerated storytelling because start-ups routinely sell their shares while still unprofitable and without solid business models. As this industry is so enthusiastic about unproven businesses, exaggeration may pay off better than anywhere else.

## CANDID VS CYNICAL

This boldness of venture capitalists is usually interpreted in one of two opposing ways. One is the candid way—VCs support courageous innovation; without them, companies like Apple wouldn't exist. The other view is the cynical one—VCs' decisions are dominated by Ponzi-like stacking of management fees and the greater fool theory. In the first couple of chapters of this book, we discussed many examples of bold investments by VCs. Their decisions were sometimes surprising and even comical, such as the support they gave to juice-pressing start-up Juicero. Let's see how both views—the candid and cynical ones—could be consistent with VCs' bold decisions.

In Chapter 1, we discussed that VCs often bet on "miracles," including start-ups that have low odds of succeeding commercially or of building their intended products. The candid explanation is that this is all part of an investment strategy based on the power law; VCs invest in big ideas because they want to win big. The cynical explanation is that, perhaps, VCs are fond of outlandish ideas that sound really big because they receive a lot of attention, and other investors are lured into them. A venture capitalist told me, "They like to generate the fear of missing out. Others see you've invested in a crazy start-up and think, 'these guys must know something,' so they want to jump onboard."

In Chapter 2, we spoke about moats, which are protective barriers required by a business to stave off competitors and generate good profits in the long run. However, we saw that VCs sometimes bet on start-ups that don't have a moat or a realistic path to build one. The candid explanation for this is that VCs expect these start-ups to find a way to establish a moat later on; after all, business strategy must always be dynamic and adapt to changing circumstances. The cynical explanation is that VCs don't care all that much about moats or long-term prospects in general, as their goal is to exit their investments early on. In fact, if there is truth to the greater fool theory, it is best to pretend that a start-up has a bigger moat than it truly does, in order to convince the next round of investors of its potential.

We also mentioned examples of fraudulent start-ups, such as Theranos and FTX, which kept receiving money from investors. The candid view is that these were unfortunate exceptions and, just like customers, VCs were duped by dishonest founders. The cynical view is that VCs' bar of due diligence has dropped quite low, as they're not in for the long run. A *Financial Times* article commented, "Doesn't anyone do due diligence anymore? ... Veteran Silicon Valley dealmakers say there has been a gradual erosion of standards."[54]

It is difficult to tell which of the two viewpoints—candid or cynical—explains the bold choices of VCs. Perhaps there's a bit of truth in both. Note that the cynical view does not imply a conscious attempt to deceive others or irrational behavior; strange investment decisions may simply be the result of VCs trying to do an efficient job by prioritizing actions that yield them the most immediate and tangible results.

## THE PAPER TRAIL

If venture capital isn't working all that well, why do people keep giving it money? The Kauffman Foundation argues, "To really understand and constructively address what's 'broken' in VC, we need to follow the money. And the money trail leads right to the LP boardroom, where investment committees oversee venture capital investing. It's in the boardroom that VC allocations are created, VC fund performance is evaluated, investment consultants are heard, and investment decisions are approved.... We wonder: why are LPs so committed to investing in VC despite its persistent underperformance?"[55]

According to the foundation, there are a few structural issues which explain continued VC investment despite poor performance. For example, the LPs' investment committee often mandates its staff to invest in VC funds: "Mandates require investment staff to invest a fixed percent of the portfolio or a fixed amount of capital into VC.... LPs with VC mandates act like the money is 'burning a hole in their pockets.' They just need to spend it." These mandates are due to overconfidence in the potential of VC returns, sometimes encouraged by consultants: "Investment consultants generate search fees and revenues for investigating and recommending venture capital firms and may have little incentive to take an independent stance against an underperforming investment." Moreover, some LPs have dedicated staff focused on VC investing. So, according to the Kauffman Foundation, "There is little incentive for those investors to alert the investment committee to the poor performance or misaligned incentives of the venture capital industry. ... After all, who wants to introduce a line of inquiry that could be job threatening?" Other people have argued that VCs' exaggeration of early returns could benefit LP staff too "as it gives them the markups and projected returns that they need to keep their own bosses happy."[56]

Moreover, it appears that LPs don't want to question the "2 and 20" compensation structure because they're afraid to ruin their relationships with VCs and be left out of good deals. The Kauffman Foundation explains, "LPs who do have access to the ten or twenty top-performing funds may not have much leverage in extracting information or negotiating better terms on their own because the line of investors waiting at the door is long." One LP even said he didn't worry about management fees because "those guys have to make a living too."

I suggest we follow the paper trail even further, well beyond LPs. Over the past few years, we've experienced a surge of cheap—or even free—money due to easy access to credit and government grants. Could that be the root of the issue?

# CHAPTER 4

# CHEAP MONEY, FREE MONEY

The scale of the 2008 financial crisis was out of the ordinary. In the U.S. and Europe, it was the most severe economic crisis since the 1930s. To help recover from the crisis, central banks around the world took an extreme measure: they lowered the cost of borrowing money, or the *interest rate*, all the way down to zero, and kept it that way for nearly a decade. This became known as *zero interest rate policy*, or ZIRP (pronounced as one word that rhymes with *burp*). ZIRP was accompanied by other colossal and unconventional policies, some of which had never been tried before and whose impacts were uncertain.

Lowering the interest rate, which is a common tool to fight recessions, has two major impacts on the economy. The first one is straightforward: It makes borrowing money cheaper. Policymakers hope that such "cheap money" will encourage businesses and households to borrow more money and spend it, which should reactivate economic activity.

The second effect is more subtle but equally important. When the interest rate goes down, lending money to the government and other safe investments stop generating good returns. Policymakers hope this will incite entrepreneurs to pursue new, uncertain lines of business, as investing safely doesn't pay off anymore. Policymakers also hope it will encourage investors to "chase yield" by moving away from safe assets and turning into riskier ones like stocks or venture capital.

Imagine you save $500,000 for retirement and that your pension fund invests it in safe assets that generate a return of 5% a year. That isn't too much to ask; two-year U.S. government bonds, for example, provided a safe 5% return to investors for decades during the twentieth century. By investing your $500,000 pension pot in those assets, you would make around $2,000 a month, perhaps enough to retire with.

Now, imagine the return on those assets suddenly dropped to 0.25% for a prolonged period of time, as was the case during ZIRP. Investing in them would only return you around $100 a month and likely ruin your retirement plans. Your fund manager, desperate to generate higher returns some other way, would probably sell off the bonds and invest the proceeds in other assets like corporate bonds and venture capital, which are expected to generate higher returns. This comes at the price of risk though, as these assets can lose you a lot of money very quickly and are highly vulnerable to fluctuations in the business landscape. By bringing interest rates close to zero, ZIRP was engineered to encourage investors to take risks; it was a feature of the policy, not a bug.

ZIRP was praised for stimulating the economy and even "nurturing innovation."[1] However, some people remained unconvinced about that; they argued that forced risk-taking could cause problems. For example, it may have fueled the "unicorn bubble" that produced the likes of Juicero and WeWork.

In this chapter, we'll first discuss the mechanism by which central banks alter the interest rate. We'll then see how it was taken to a whole new level through a controversial policy known as *quantitative easing*. After that, we'll ask ourselves whether these policies could have contributed to the unicorn boom of the 2010s and early 2020s. Next, we'll observe that some unorthodox economists had been warning us all along that these policies could cause harm. We'll finally explore how, with the goal of encouraging innovation, some governments have provided large quantities of "free" money to tech start-ups, which they didn't have to pay back, perhaps fueling the bubble even further.

## UNCONVENTIONAL METHODS

If it were left to its own means, the interest rate would be determined by market forces. It would be the price of loans agreed on by lenders and borrowers based on their preferences. However, central banks, such as the U.S. Federal Reserve ("the Fed"), the Bank of England, and the European Central Bank, intervene in loan markets to alter the market-determined interest rate.

When people speak of *the* interest rate, they usually mean the rate of very safe, short-term loans not available to the general public. In the U.S., for example, it refers to the *federal funds rate*, which is the rate at which commercial banks borrow money from one another, which sometimes banks need to do in order to fulfill their obligations and comply with regulation. Such is the rate on which the Fed sets a target.

The interest rate affects the wider economy because it sets a baseline on the interest rate of all sorts of loans and the returns generated by all sorts of assets. For example, safe assets tend to generate returns for investors that closely match the federal funds rate, so they're very sensitive to its fluctuations. Such is the case, for example, with short-term government bonds, which are loans made to the government which are sold in public markets and entitle the holder to receive the repayment of the loan by the government a short time later.

One of the mechanisms used by the Fed to lower the federal funds rate is to regularly buy assets owned by commercial banks like HSBC. The Fed typically buys safe assets like the short-term government bonds we just described. The Fed pays above-market prices for such bonds to incite banks to sell them. After selling their bonds to the Fed, commercial banks find themselves with more money in their vaults, so they become more willing to make loans to one another, which lowers the federal funds rate. Mission accomplished.

During ZIRP, bond purchases were performed at a huge scale to drop the interest rate all the way down to zero. As a consequence, the return on safe assets also dropped to near zero, pushing investors away from them. But policymakers wanted to go a step further in trying to reactivate the economy. They thought, "What if we could also reduce the returns generated by *riskier* assets?" Doing so would encourage investors to sell off risky assets to buy even riskier ones. Yay!

Central banks around the world implemented a colossal and unprecedented policy to accomplish that, which soon became known as *quantitative easing,* or QE. The policy consisted in repeatedly purchasing huge quantities of risky assets, instead of the usual short-term bonds, in order to increase their prices and thus lower the returns the public could make from them. For example, the Fed bought a huge quantity of long-term government bonds, which are loans to the government that are only paid back years later. It also bought a large quantity of mortgage-backed securities, which were the "tainted" assets that had caused the 2008 financial crisis.

Instead of buying these assets from commercial banks, central banks bought them directly from institutional investors, hoping they would immediately use the proceeds to buy riskier assets. The Bank of England explained, "Purchases have been targeted towards long-term assets held by non-bank financial institutions, like insurers and pension funds, who may be encouraged to use the funds to invest in other, riskier assets like corporate bonds and equities."[2]

QE was performed at a dramatic scale. In a 2011 article, economists from the Fed explained:

> Between December 2008 and March 2010, the Federal Reserve purchased more than $1.7 trillion in assets. This represents 22 percent of the $7.7 trillion stock of longer-term agency debt, fixed-rate agency mortgage-backed securities, and Treasury securities outstanding. ... We believe that no investor—public or private—has ever accumulated such a large amount of securities in such a short period of time.[3]

And that was just the beginning. The ZIRP and QE programs continued at a massive scale for years and were implemented by major central banks around the globe, including the Bank of England and the European Central Bank.

In 2015, it seemed that these unconventional methods could soon come to an end, as the Fed increased the federal funds rate from around zero to 2.4% and stopped QE purchases. The Bank of England, however, kept the interest rate below 0.75% and continued QE over the next few years. The European Central Bank implemented a *negative* interest rate policy, in which it charged a fee to commercial banks for not extending enough credit to customers, hoping this would encourage banks to lend more money to the public. This strange and unprecedented maneuver was the epitome of unconventional policy.

In 2020, as a response to the COVID-19 pandemic, ZIRP and QE programs were resumed by the U.S. and ramped up around the world. This time, however, QE was on steroids. Numbers speak for themselves:[4]

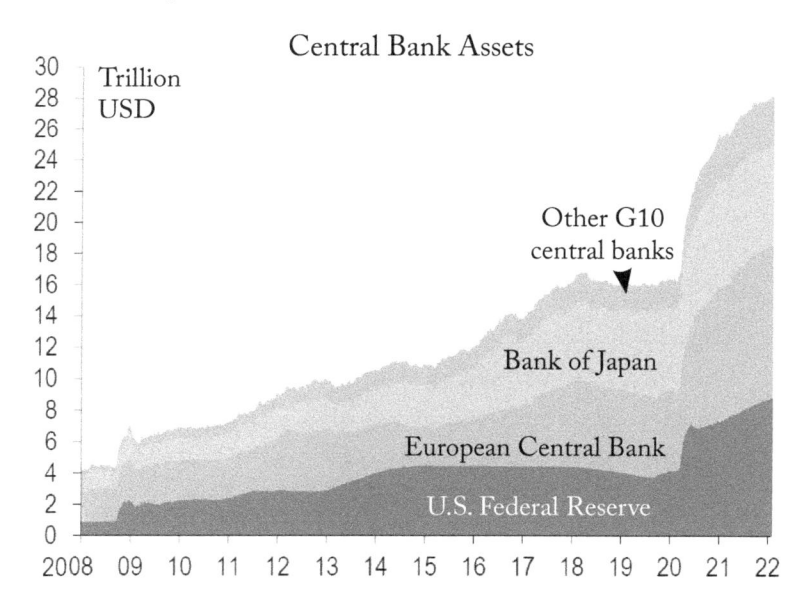

Central Bank Assets (Trillion USD), 2008–2022: Other G10 central banks, Bank of Japan, European Central Bank, U.S. Federal Reserve.

As we can see in the graph, the assets owned by central banks, which had already grown a lot since 2008 due to QE, exploded in 2020. A report by the International Monetary Fund (IMF) explained, "The combined scale of unconventional interventions [due to COVID-19] was truly staggering, since, by IMF estimates, they amounted to $7.5 trillion globally."[5]

During the pandemic, unconventional policies became even more unconventional than before. The Bank of England, for example, bought billions of bonds issued by private companies instead of the usual government bonds.[6]

Where did central banks get all that money to purchase such a huge amount of assets? They created it—out of thin air. As most money in today's banking system is just a record in a digital database, creating new money to fund QE purchases was simply performed by replacing numbers with higher numbers inside computers. Suppose, for example, that the Fed purchased bonds from a pension fund and that the pension fund had a checking account at HSBC. After a few coordinated keystrokes between HSBC and the Fed, the available balance in the pension fund's checking account at HSBC was magically changed in order to pay for the bonds—all this required was modifying a few numbers stored in databases at the Fed and HSBC. This effectively created new money that the pension fund could use for something else.[7]

Newly created money could circulate in the economy. For example, the pension fund could invest part of its newly added bank balance in venture capital. The venture capital firm could then transfer that money to a start-up, which could use it to pay coders' wages and buy beanbags.

Here's the total balances held in checking accounts in the U.S. over the years:[8]

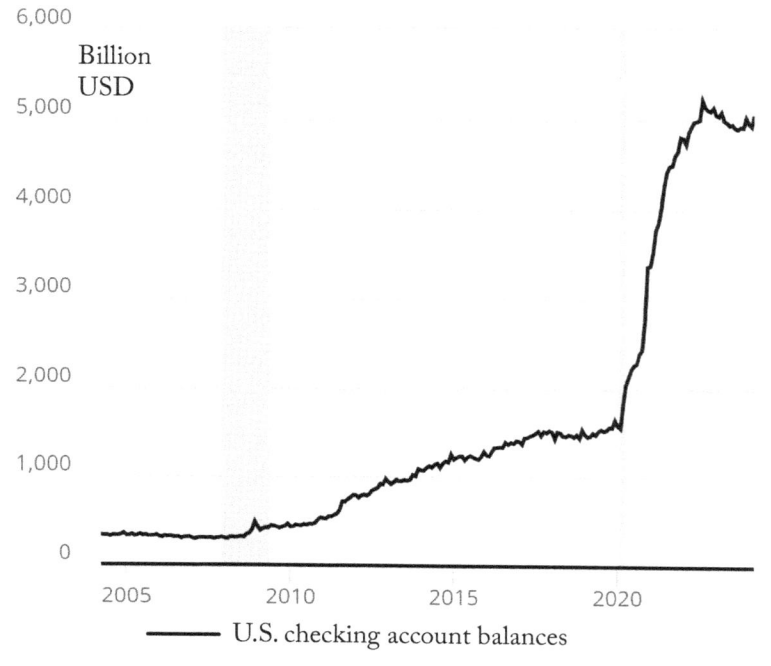

```
6,000
     Billion
     USD
5,000

4,000

3,000

2,000

1,000

   0
     2005      2010      2015      2020
        ——— U.S. checking account balances
```

We can see in the graph that balances started to grow rapidly after 2008, when QE started creating new money to fund asset purchases. It then spiked dramatically during the pandemic, as QE reached an unprecedented scale. While other factors affected these balances during the pandemic, such as increased saving and loan taking, the new money created through QE was a major contributor to the spike.[9]

An increase in the stock of money circulating in the economy tends to cause fear of inflation because an abundance of money makes it less valuable in the long run. This worried some economists. However, inflation remained stable during the first few years of QE, which made policymakers confident about the policy. Some people argued, however, that inflation remained low because the newly created balances were injected into financial institutions instead of the general public. This caused an increase in the price of financial assets instead of causing an increase in the price of, say, lettuce.[10] Some economists insisted that household products would necessarily suffer from inflation later on as the new money made its way to the wider economy.[11]

In 2021, inflation soared around the world. Economists provided a wide variety of explanations for it, ranging from the war in Ukraine to the disruption of supply chains due to the pandemic. Some people even blamed it on corporate greed, calling the phenomenon "greedflation."[12] Others weren't convinced by these explanations. Former governor of the Bank of England Mervyn King said that central banks should have asked, "If we keep printing money at this rate, what will happen?" According to King, "The answer is obvious: you'll get inflation."[13]

In 2022, central banks decided to take action to tame inflation. They started selling off assets they'd accumulated during QE and destroying some of the newly created money. They also steeply increased the interest rate. In the U.S., for example, the federal funds rate jumped from near zero to over 5% within a year. All of a sudden, the policies of government-sponsored risk-taking came to an end. This caused the crash of the tech sector.

## THE UNICORN BOOM (AND BUST)

By the early 2010s, the internet had become massively adopted. This led to the surge of a new kind of start-up whose main value proposition was to connect people with one another.

Technology commentator Tom Goodwin explains, "Uber, the world's largest taxi company, owns no vehicles. Facebook, the world's most popular media owner, creates no content. Alibaba, the most valuable retailer, has no inventory. And Airbnb, the world's largest accommodation provider, owns no real estate. Something interesting is happening."[14]

This model proved successful for many start-ups, which grew really fast and benefited from powerful network effects, which protected them from competitors. Thanks to their impressive prospects, many of them quickly reached billion-dollar valuations. As no other line of business promised such outstanding results, investors became highly enthusiastic about the sector. But enthusiasm alone isn't usually enough; investors must have access to funds, and they must be convinced that the risk is worth taking.

Many people believe that the unconventional economic policies of the 2010s provided the fuel that powered the boom. Technology reporter Alex Hern explains:

> With low rates of return from conventional investments, the venture capital ecosystem—one of the few legitimate financial products that tries to offer a thousand-fold return on investment—became flush with cash. Yes, the risk was high, but with [interest] rates so low it was a risk that was worth taking. … Free sushi lunches? That's a ZIRP phenomenon. Massive discounts for new users? ZIRP phenomenon. Burning money on a metaverse? Definite ZIRP phenomenon.[15]

According to a *Financial Times* article, the size of VC investments increased due to "decades of easy money and a lack of decent yields from safer alternatives," which made VCs go from "small investment rounds involving a few million dollars to gigantic deals involving billions."[16] This sentiment soon became commonplace. A *Wall Street Journal* article described the tech boom as a "sugar high of free money,"[17] and a *CNBC* article stated, "Investors, hungry for yield, poured into the riskiest areas of tech. ... The mania reached a zenith in 2021."[18] Note that the 2021 zenith coincided with the steepest increase in newly created checking account balances in history and the sudden return of the U.S. to ZIRP due to COVID-19.

Low interest rates also provided cheap credit which fueled VC activity. For example, the Silicon Valley Bank, or SVB, provided billions in credit to VC firms to let them invest in start-ups *before* the LPs provided the necessary funds for it, which made the process quicker; almost half of the bank's loans consisted of this type of credit. Moreover, SVB lent money to VC firms to help them pay in their own contributions to the funds (if you remember, VCs typically invest some of their own money into their funds, typically 1% of the fund, to have more skin in the game). A *Bloomberg* article explains, "Partners could turn to SVB for personal loans that gave them additional money to invest alongside their clients even as fund sizes expanded into the billions and fundraising cycles accelerated."[19]

When interest rates rose in 2022, investment into start-ups collapsed as safer assets became more appealing.[20] By the end of 2023, it reached a six-year low and stood at 40% of the 2021 spike. Start-ups require continued investment to survive, so the lack of new investments made many of them short of cash and put their future in jeopardy.

Many VC-funded start-ups had their main bank accounts with SVB—a whopping 50% of them in the U.S. and 30% in the U.K. A reporter explained that this was due to the "difficulty in opening accounts at high street banks—and investors' cozy relationship with SVB."[21] After the 2022 downturn, balances with SVB started to drop because start-ups continued spending their money while not receiving the same inflow of investments.

The bank soon found itself short of cash to fund start-ups' withdrawals. So, it had to start selling off its assets.[22] But the bank had invested in risky assets whose prices had dropped significantly, so it had to sell them at a loss. The bank announced it would try to raise money from the public by selling a new batch of shares. This announcement triggered a bank run, meaning that many panicked customers tried to withdraw their deposits at the same time, which the impoverished SVB couldn't honor. As a result, SVB collapsed; it was the largest bank failure in the U.S. since 2008. The bank was acquired by HSBC UK for the symbolic sum of one British pound, and customers' deposits were secured.

As the tech crash unfolded, start-ups started failing at record rates, and the amount of money generated by exits dropped from $797 billion in 2021 to $61.5 billion in 2023.[23] The unicorn boom didn't turn out as expected.

## WHACK-A-MOLE

If you're old enough to have been to an arcade, you may remember a coin-operated game called whack-a-mole. In this game, mole-shaped plastic figures popped up from holes in a cabinet, and you had to punch them. As the game progressed, moles started popping up more frequently, making it harder to hit them. Recent events have made some people believe that policies like ZIRP are a whack-a-mole way of managing the economy; they only solve problems superficially and perhaps even cause other problems to pop up elsewhere.

Let's travel back to the U.S. in the late 1990s. The country hadn't experienced a major financial bubble since the 1920s, and the economy had been stable since 1985, which became known as the Great Moderation. During that time, the internet started to expand explosively, which caused enormous enthusiasm among investors. Enthusiasm was justified, as the new technology proved life-changing, but it seemed a little exaggerated as people paid eye-watering prices for shares of tech companies that weren't even profitable. This became known as the dot-com bubble. While the rise of the internet may have triggered all that enthusiasm, a bubble needs fuel to grow. Financial historian William Quinn explains, "The fuel for the bubble is money and credit. A bubble can form only when the public has sufficient capital to invest in the asset and is therefore much more likely to occur when there is abundant money and credit in the economy."[24]

In 1998, the economic landscape became a bit more challenging as a series of crises in Asia caused market turmoil. These crises led to the collapse of a large U.S. hedge fund called Long-Term Capital Management. Fearing a recession, the Fed organized a bailout of the fund by other banks and lowered the interest rate from 5.5% to 4.75% to stimulate the economy. Some people believe that such lowering of the interest rate provided fuel for the dot-com bubble to grow.[25] Moreover, some of the Fed's past actions made investors think the Fed would "rescue" them with low interest rates if tech stock prices dropped, which provided additional fuel.[26] In addition, it became common to borrow money to purchase shares, a practice that increased by 144% during the period, which provided even more fuel.[27]

In March 2000, as enthusiasm proved exaggerated, the dot-com bubble burst. As a result, the Fed decided to hold interest rates at 6.5% for nearly a year, a level not seen in a decade, in order to cool off the economy and clean up the mess. This didn't last though.

The dot-com crash triggered a recession, and policymakers decided to fight it using their favorite tool: lower interest rates. The drop was dramatic—from 6.5% to 1.75% in 2001, then down to 1.25% by the end of 2002, and then down to 1% six months later, a level not observed since 1958. The rate was held at 1% for a year and only increased very slowly thereafter, which resulted in a prolonged period of incentivized risk-taking. But this policy may have had unintended consequences. Economist Robert D. Murphy jokingly said that policymakers "prescribed a housing bubble as a solution to the dot-com crash."[28]

The low interest rate policy came at the same time as financial innovations made it easier for banks to extend mortgages, as they started pooling many mortgages together and selling them as a package to others. Low interest rates coupled with easier access to credit provided the fuel to a housing boom of epic proportions. During the boom, the yearly number of newly built houses increased by 20% in the U.S.,[29] which led to a whopping 1.47 new houses per new inhabitant.[30] Disproportionate housing booms were also observed around the world, notably in the U.K., Ireland, and Spain.

When the housing market crashed in 2008, policymakers decided to fight the recession by doubling down on low interest rates, and the era of ZIRP and QE started. As already discussed, this may have fueled the tech boom of the 2010s and early 2020s; perhaps a unicorn bubble was part of the medicine that policymakers prescribed for the housing crash.

It seems that cheap money has repeatedly salvaged the economy. But it also seems that it has caused other problems to pop up faster than before, reminding us of the game of whack-a-mole. The cure has also been more draconian each time, going from a low interest rate to a lower interest rate, to a zero interest rate. Is it possible that cheap money leads to unsustainable booms? Could it be akin to a partygoer who abuses the open bar only to regret it the morning after?

## HANGOVER THEORIES

Over the twentieth century, economists studied the repeated ups and downs in economy activity, known as the *business cycle,* and developed competing theories to explain the phenomenon. Over time, the different theories were somehow integrated into a common framework known as the New Synthesis,[31] which is widely accepted today. This framework, which is the current mainstream economics framework, guides contemporary policymakers.

The framework asserts that the "busts" of the business cycle are caused by unpredictable shocks of various kinds. One kind of shock, for example, is the demand shock, which happens when businesses suddenly lose confidence in the future and reduce their investment, sending the economy on a downward spiral. Another type of shock is the supply shock, which happens when the price of an important good, like oil, increases sharply. Other shocks, such as unexpected changes in monetary policy or technological innovation are also accepted as sources of economic fluctuations.

There exist, however, alternative theories of the business cycle, which are part of heterodox, or "non-mainstream" schools of economics. Two prominent examples are the Austrian school and the post-Keynesian school. The reason I'm bringing them up is that, contrary to mainstream theories, they both suggest that some economic booms are predictably unsustainable and plant the seeds of their own destruction; the boom brews the bust. Some people have mockingly called these ideas "hangover theories." In light of recent events, it is perhaps worth revisiting them.

The Austrian theory of the business cycle was developed by Ludwig von Mises and Friedrich Hayek in the 1920s. The theory says that an artificially low interest rate due to central bank intervention causes an unsustainable boom, which ends up in a crash. You can see why I'm bringing this up.

The theory says that an artificially low interest rate causes *malinvestment*—entrepreneurs spend too much on long-term projects while people don't save much for future consumption. Ultimately, entrepreneurs can't generate enough profit to justify their long-term investments.[32] A hypothetical example for the tech era could be as follows: Due to the low interest rate, venture capitalists invest in a plethora of food delivery and e-bike start-ups, only to discover later on that dissaved consumers end up cooking at home and riding ordinary bikes more than expected.

According to the Austrian school of thought, if policymakers try to fight an economic downturn by doubling down on a low interest rate policy, they risk making the problem worse. Back in 1946, an Austrian-leaning journalist warned, "An artificial reduction in the interest rate encourages increased borrowing. It tends, in fact, to encourage highly speculative ventures that cannot continue except under the artificial conditions that gave them birth. ... Cheap money policies, in short, eventually bring about far more violent oscillations in business than those they are designed to remedy or prevent."[33]

The post-Keynesian school of thought is inspired by a theory formulated by economist John Maynard Keynes in the 1930s, which argues that our economies can easily get stuck for prolonged periods of time. In the spirit of Keynes, post-Keynesians argue that our economies are inefficient and unstable, and they reject more recent theories that say economies tend to self-equilibrate. Within this school of thought, in the 1970s, economist Hyman Minsky formulated the *financial instability hypothesis*, which is a "hangover" theory of the business cycle. This theory states that during good times, businesses and banks become confident because they notice that loans are repaid promptly. So, they become less careful about borrowing and lending money, and this optimism leads to an excessive expansion of credit. At the height of the boom, some businesses take so much credit that they need new credit to pay the interest on old credit, which Minsky called "Ponzi finance." After a while, overly indebted businesses cannot fulfill their obligations and fail. After the crash, panicked lenders and borrowers become more conservative and thus lending becomes much safer, which triggers a new episode of boom and bust.

These two schools of economics—Austrian and Post-Keynesian—never made it to the mainstream. However, they've regained attention the past few years, especially after the 2008 crisis.[34] Some people even called the 2008 crisis a "Minsky moment."[35] Let's discuss why these theories haven't become popular and why, perhaps, they should.

## NASTY FIGHTS

Until the 1970s, many economic models assumed people were easy to dupe and made decisions against their best interests. For example, economists routinely estimated the effects of a certain policy assuming people would not change their behavior as a result of the policy. This made policymakers overly confident of the impact of their actions. In 1976, Robert Lucas severely criticized these practices in an influential paper, which revolutionized the profession.[36] Since then, mainstream economists have embraced *rationality*, the idea that individuals make decisions in their best interests and with a good understanding of the impact of policy. Rationality has become so engrained in mainstream economics that many economists reject that a "bubble" can happen at all—why would rational investors buy overvalued assets? And, if investors can identify a bubble, then why doesn't it pop immediately? For those reasons, economist Eugene Fama said, "The word 'bubble' drives me nuts."[37] The strong confidence in rationality may be the reason why economists weren't too bothered by the decade of ZIRP and QE; they didn't expect rational businesses to act in a self-destructive way as a result of these policies.

Rationality is one of the main reasons mainstream economists reject the Austrian and post-Keynesian theories. They argue that these theories imply that businesses are irrational, as they keep making the same mistakes over and over. For example, why would entrepreneurs repeatedly make unsustainable investments when interest rates are low, like the Austrians say? The same goes for Minsky's idea—why would borrowers and lenders become overconfident in good times, if this is known to cause problems?

Austrians have responded to this objection by saying that it is costly for businesses to conduct thorough investigations about the state of the economy. So, it might be perfectly rational for businesses that have limited resources to deprioritize thoroughly analyzing the wide economy.[38] A start-up, for example, may focus its efforts on fundraising to stay afloat instead of, say, calculating whether customers have been saving enough to afford its products in the long run. Moreover, many companies don't build final products ready for consumption; instead, they build a piece of a product in a long value chain that involves many other companies. In those cases, it's hard to know whether a long-term project is sustainable in the long run, as the final consumers are very far along the value chain.

Post-Keynesians are also skeptical that rationality threatens their theories of financial instability. They often stress out that the future is genuinely uncertain,[39] so borrowers and lenders have no way to build a truly rational expectation about lending risk. Instead, they rely on the recent past to estimate risk because they don't have much of a choice.

Moreover, note that some apparently irrational actions may actually be optimal for those who make them, even if they aren't good for others. For example, as we discussed before, VCs may focus their efforts on raising more and more funds instead of making good investments because that maximizes their profits thanks to management fees. As writer an activist Upton Sinclair once said, "It is difficult to get a man to understand something, when his salary depends on his not understanding it."[40]

Moreover, if businesses suspect they'll be bailed out when they're in trouble, as has been the case before, taking high risks may be the rational thing to do. Back in 1978, Minsky warned, "Once the doctrine of salvation through investment becomes deeply ingrained into our political and economic system the constraints on foolish investment are relaxed. This is especially so if the government stands ready to guarantee particular investors or investment projects against losses."[41]

In addition to rationality, multiple other objections have been raised against Austrian and post-Keynesian theories. For example, some people argue that the Austrian theory is not supported by empirical evidence. Austrians respond to this by saying that these arguments rely on overly aggregated data, such as unemployment across the entire economy, which obscures the mechanics of individual booming sectors like housing.[42] Mainstream economists remain unconvinced, and the back and forth between passionate supporters and detractors of the Austrian theory is still ongoing.

Minsky's financial instability hypothesis has also been criticized on many fronts. A common attack is that, even if an overconfident company borrows money recklessly, that money is spent elsewhere in the economy, which could be beneficial to other firms and reduce instability. Supporters of Minsky's theory argue that instability is still possible in the financial system as a whole and that such a refutation is "based entirely on theory since empirical data seem to prove that Minsky was right."[43] Just like in the Austrian case, passionate debate is still ongoing.

The back and forth between mainstream and non-mainstream economists is often highly unpleasant, as the different camps ridicule and insult each other. For example, mainstream economist Paul Krugman said that the Austrian theory was "as worthy of serious study as the phlogiston theory of fire" and added that the theory explained recessions as "a necessary punishment ... turning into morality play, a tale of hubris and downfall."[44] Non-mainstream economists have become equally scornful of their counterparts. For example, post-Keynesian economist Steve Keen tells the following story:

> I was presenting my model of Minsky's financial instability hypothesis at the Western Economic Association Conference. ... I was expecting an 'irrational' reaction from this young zealot to my talk. And bingo! Unable to restrain himself, he blurted out 'But you're assuming people are idiots!' in the middle of my talk. I then asked him, 'Well, did you predict the Great Recession?', to which he replied, rather querulously, 'Um, no.' I then said, 'So by your own definition you're an idiot. Why shouldn't I model the world as being made up of people like you?'[45]

An economist told me that Austrians and Post-Keynesians often propose extremely radical solutions to fix the economy, which makes it hard for others to hear them out. For example, some Austrians support the elimination of central banks, a return to the gold standard, and the wide adoption of cryptocurrencies. Their post-Keynesians counterparts support equally draconian policies, such as giving huge quantities of newly printed money to citizens and businesses to help them pay off their debts,[46] which they call "the people's quantitative easing."

At the same time, mainstream economists have been accused of clinging too hard to their ideas while being intolerant to alternatives.[47] Moreover, they've often endorsed and taught incorrect explanations of how the economy works. For example, as of today, most economics' textbooks explain the mechanics of bank lending the wrong way around; they say banks lend out their reserves to customers when in reality, banks create new money when they extend loans and destroy it when loans are repaid, so lending doesn't change the amount of reserves inside banks' vaults. Non-mainstream economists complained about this for years to no avail. In 2014, the Bank of England published an article debunking the textbook explanation.[48]

None of this is new, however. Stern defense of one's position and disregard for those of others have been features of economics since the 1930s.[49] Perhaps the time has come for the different schools of thought to talk to one another and try to find a "New New Synthesis." If not, we may prescribe the wrong medicine over and over.

## IS IT WORTH IT?

The policies of cheap money have been praised by many. A *Financial Times* article explains, "Basically, easier monetary policy tends to stimulate R&D bonanzas, stir VC splurges and nurture innovation, while tighter monetary policy does the reverse. And all that innovation tends to enhance the productivity and potential of an economy (in addition to the more obvious near-term impact of lower interest rates). In other words: bubbles should be praised!"[50]

I reached out to financial historian William Quinn, who specializes in economic bubbles, and asked him whether bubbles could have benefits. He told me:

> A good example is the ESG bubble [environmental, social, and corporate governance]. These environmentally

friendly assets, or asset classes that sold themselves as environmentally friendly, were very overvalued as investments, and this became known as the ESG bubble. I think to a large extent it was for show, as supposedly ESG companies included Exxon, but if we set that aside we'd be saying that firms using green technology were finding it much easier to raise money cheaply, and clearly that's a good thing from an environmentalist perspective. Another example is the dot-com bubble, as for a few years the most innovative sector of the economy found it very, very easy to raise money. Again, that's a good thing.

I then asked him whether bubbles were worth it. He said:

I don't really think in terms of worth it or not worth it. It's just what happened. There can be a situation where the benefits outweigh the costs, for sure. But it's hard to know because in order to answer that question you would need a counterfactual. You would need to answer, "If there wasn't a bubble, what would have happened instead?" It's very hard to assess the benefits and costs.

Indeed, while bubbles may have benefits, they also have costs. This includes the hidden cost of not using valuable resources for something else. For example, if juice-pressing start-up Juicero hadn't been launched, perhaps its coveted engineers would have been employed for more useful projects instead. Or would they have been unemployed? As we can't go back in time and rerun an alternative course of history, this is very hard to know.

I then asked Quinn for his policy recommendations. He answered:

> I tend to think that the best solution is to protect the financial sector. Bubbles cause a serious problem whenever the banks are involved. Another thing that can be done is protect vulnerable investors. This is what an institution like the SEC should be doing. I find in the technology world that there's this sort of spectrum between what's acceptable and what's not—there's "fake it till you make it," and there's also Theranos. Some kind of investor protection needs to happen there.

## FREE MONEY

A few years ago, a start-up reached out to me with a crazy product idea intended to revolutionize commercial aviation. The product was a platform on which airlines could "steal" passengers from one another. For example, suppose a passenger booked a flight with airline A. The airline would publish the booking details on this platform for others to see. Airline B could make a better offer to the passenger, such as a cheaper ticket on the same route. If the passenger accepted the offer, airline A would cancel the reservation and airline B would acquire the customer. In exchange, airline A could equally take customers from other airlines by using the same mechanism.

The idea belonged to the "miracle" category, as it was extremely unlikely an airline would ever agree to having its customers poached by another one. The flights market has become so competitive that airlines try to retain every single customer; that's why they rarely offer refundable fares and don't even let passengers transfer a reservation to someone else.

The start-up decided to apply for a government grant to help it fund this project. The program, called Horizon 2020, was run by the European Union and funded by the taxpayer for a budget of 80 billion euros. If a start-up won the grant, it did *not* have to pay the money back, ever. To the start-up, this was effectively "free" money. The grant didn't come with many strings; the start-up just had to meet a government official once in a while and file a report summarizing the project's outcome much later.

My job was to help the start-up write the grant application, which was a long report detailing the intended project. The biggest challenge of the grant application was describing the intended product without raising questions abouts its viability. My approach was to hide its weaknesses in plain sight. I wrote an easy-to-follow, confident explanation of the mechanics of the intended platform. I hoped this would make grant reviewers comfortable, and they would refrain from scrutiny.

The second-biggest challenge was proving that our product was aligned with at least one of the major societal goals of the European Union, which we heard was essential to win the grant. The most notable goal was environmental sustainability, to which 60% of the grant money would be allocated. In the application I argued that our product would help reduce the number of empty seats on flights, which would make flying more eco-friendly. I mentioned this environmental benefit within a long list of other, unrelated benefits, without highlighting it enthusiastically. I thought this would help grant reviewers tick the sustainability box without raising too many questions.

The European Union approved the grant right away, and we received the money almost immediately. A point of contact within the European Union asked us which consulting company we'd hired to write the application for us, which apparently was a big thing. When we told him it was all us, he was quite surprised. I don't know whether I should be proud of my achievement. In 2021, the European Union renewed the program for seven years, which it renamed Horizon Europe, with a budget of 95.5 million euros.

Similar government programs, which give free money to start-ups, abound around the world; they exist in the U.K., France, Finland, Austria, Australia, and Japan, to name a few.[51] In the U.K., for example, the government's innovation agency gives a combined 25 million pounds of free money to start-ups every quarter. Lately, there's been a proliferation of consulting companies in the U.K. which help start-ups write their applications for that grant. These companies guide start-ups on what to say and how to say it in order to tick all the right boxes. If the grant is approved, they charge the start-up a percentage of the grant's money. Some also charge a flat fee on top independently of the outcome.

One may wonder why governments give grants to start-ups to build commercial products—why not let them raise funding through the usual channels, such as venture capital? The government's rationale for it is that the private sector may "under-invest" due to being overly cautious, and grants can help fill in the investment gap. A study of government grants explains:

> Innovative activities, especially front-end R&D, are very risky, indivisible and often excessively costly. Thus, there

is risk that the investment to the innovative activity might not be as desired (profitable) as possible for actors to persuade them to invest. In combination, these features ultimately lead to the risk of under-investment since the private optimum level of innovative activity could be less than the social optimum level.[52]

While grants may foster innovation sometimes, they also create distortions. One common type of distortion is that grants may end up funding projects that would have received funding anyway by private investors. So, a level of risk that the private sector was willing to bear may end up being borne by the taxpayer.

A U.K. government website claims that its grant program has created thousands of new jobs and generated £5 for every £1 invested.[53] But is that so?

These promising figures were extracted from a study conducted by a consulting company hired to independently assess the grant program. I wanted to understand how this was all calculated, but the report was no longer available on the website. So, I sent an email to request a copy through the official Freedom of Information channel. A government employee denied the request:

> The link to the report on our website should have been removed, and it is pending action. To be clear, as this evaluation has been withdrawn we are no longer able to share the published findings unfortunately, except for the summary of the findings that remains on the link you have already shared with us.

I ended up coming across a copy of the report elsewhere.[54]

The results were surprising. While the report concluded that the grant program had created jobs, it also revealed much less flattering results which weren't announced by the government. For example, 40% of the companies which received the grant admitted that they would have been able to pursue their projects anyway without taking that money. And of the companies which did *not* obtain the grant but were very close to it, 57% still had managed to pursue their projects. The report states, "Arguably there is a need to more rigorously test the genuine need for [grant] finance at the application and assessment stage."

Various studies of other grant programs have revealed similar results, with 15–66% of grant beneficiaries saying they thought they still would have been able to pursue their projects without the government's help.[55] And an evaluation of an Austrian grant revealed that 10–15% of projects which requested the grant but didn't obtain it went on with their projects without the slightest delay or modification, suggesting the money wasn't needed at all in the first place. The report stated that these companies were attempting to "free ride" on the subsidy.[56]

Another distortion caused by government grants is that in order to increase the quantity of projects funded, the government may have to drop the quality bar pretty low; after all, the goal of government grants is precisely to fund projects that the private sector deems not good enough. Back in 1946, journalist Henry Hazlitt warned, "The proposal is frequently made that the government ought to assume the risks that are 'too great for private industry.' This means that bureaucrats should be permitted to take risks with the taxpayers' money that no one is willing to take with his own."[57]

Governments tend to measure and promote the success of their grant programs by how many projects they've supported or how much money they've distributed; they rarely quantify or report the long-term success of these projects. Perhaps this encourages government officials to focus on quantity rather than quality, as my airline story may suggest, because there may be no negative consequences for supporting projects with poor prospects.

Note that grants weren't suspended during the unicorn boom, when VC funding was at an all-time high. During that time, companies with outlandish ideas like Juicero secured funding from private investors. How low did the bar have to drop for the government to fund projects that the private sector deemed too risky?

Yet another distortion is that entrepreneurs may not always use grant money wisely, as it is free and comes with few strings compared to private funding. For example, I've come across start-ups which use grant money in a completely different way than promised in the grant application; one start-up allocated the money to call center staff as opposed to innovative research.

Another common way in which governments try to foster innovation is to protect investors' losses. For example, one such program in the U.K. is the Seed Enterprise Investment Scheme, or SEIS, which helps private individuals invest in start-ups directly. Suppose a wealthy individual invests £100,000 in a start-up. If the start-up fails, instead of losing the entire sum, SEIS lets the investor obtain a refund of £72,500 in the form of tax relief on other sources of income. So, the investor can only suffer a maximum loss of £27,500 from the £100,000 investment. In addition, if things go well, all gains are tax free. The dramatic protection against losses and the potential for unlimited, tax-free gains makes this a very appealing proposition.

While this program is intended to promote innovation, it has unintended consequences. For example, I recently met the manager of a venture capital fund which, instead of investing the fund's money directly into start-ups, operates as a matchmaker. The manager selects start-ups and introduces them to wealthy individuals who invest "directly" into them, which allows them to benefit from SEIS. The VC fund obtains shares of the start-up separately as payment for the matchmaking service.

The manager of this fund told me that wealthy individuals seemed extremely eager to invest in start-ups this way, as the deal was really good for them. Apparently, they weren't too picky when choosing start-ups because their risk was largely protected. Some of them told the manager they'd rather invest their money quickly in a random start-up through SEIS than "throw it out" by making a more cautious but unprotected investment. One of them even told him that if he lost a bit of money but could tell a good story about his involvement in the start-up, the resulting PR would make the small loss worth it.

The policies of cheap and free money are meant to encourage economic activity and innovation. It is very hard to argue against that—who would want to say that the economy should be given a smaller nudge or entrepreneurs should receive less help? But let's not forget that these policies may have other, unintended consequences.

Propelled by cheap and free money, the tech sector has received unimaginable amounts of funds—sometimes hundreds of billions in a single year. But has this money been used for productive endeavors, keeping talented tech employees very busy working on real things? Let's see.

# CHAPTER 5

# RECIPES FOR UNPRODUCTIVITY

In March 2023, I resigned from a high-paying technology job. The reason was that I struggled to find any work to do, so I was idle and bored most of the time. I had been excited to join this company, as I'd be part of a cutting-edge technology project. On my first day, however, they told me I'd be "on the bench" for a while, together with another ten new recruits, waiting until they found me work to do. In the meantime, I'd be paid my full salary. I was worried about my situation, so I followed up every few days, and the company kept apologizing and promising they'd soon give me something to do.

After three months of idleness, I finally joined a team. However, I soon realized that the team was severely overstaffed; there wasn't enough work for everyone. So, my colleagues split simple tasks into tiny subtasks and pretended to work on them for weeks. My job was also to pretend. Over the following three months, I worked perhaps a total of three hours.

My boss sensed I wasn't happy and asked what he could do to improve my situation. I told him there didn't seem to be enough work for everyone in the team, so perhaps he could find me a different one. He told me there was another team within the larger project that could be a good fit. When I met the team members to discuss their work, they all seemed very demotivated. They explained to me that they were building a product that would never be used—it would be scrapped in a month or so—but they were still improving it because otherwise they'd have nothing else to do. I decided to leave the company at that point.

If that was the only time I'd experienced something like this, I would have thought it was an exception. However, this was the last of a series of jobs where I was hired not to work. This had happened to me both in tech companies and in tech teams within non-tech companies and both in start-ups and established businesses. In one of those jobs, one of my colleagues once told the rest of the team over dinner, "We haven't produced anything in two years. When do you guys think they'll get rid of our team?" In other cases, I did find work to do, but it involved building experimental products that would likely never be used, which made work feel pointless. I began to suspect that something really strange was happening in the industry.

I started speaking about this situation with others and soon discovered that a lot of techies around me were also idle. One of my friends, for example, had two full-time tech jobs at the same time, as neither kept him too busy. This was a secret; neither employer knew about the existence of the other. He'd been doing that for five years. His employers paid him tech-level, six-figure salaries, so he saved a lot of money. A few years back, he even held three jobs simultaneously for a few months, but it was too stressful to keep the secret, so he quit one of them and stuck with two ever since.

I also found out that another high-paid techie friend of mine was working very little; all she did was prepare a PowerPoint presentation every week. Another friend, who was employed by an AI start-up, only worked fifteen minutes a day. He told me they seemed to keep him around just in case because he had a PhD in AI, and his skillset could become useful one day.

I then met a former colleague, who now worked for an AI team within a famous tech company. He told me his team had been overstaffed soon after he joined, so there was very little work for him to do. He spent most of his office hours watching online courses on Coursera in the office. He told me he'd consider resigning if the company canceled its subscription to Coursera. I also met a former colleague who, last time I checked, was working quite intensely for a video-editing start-up. But now, as the start-up had overstaffed the team, he had little to do. While he was still a full-time employee for the company, he dedicated his work hours to a personal project—a brick-and-mortar hospitality business.

Another friend was hired to write stock-trading software for one of the world's most important investment banks. The interview process was among the hardest you can imagine—brain teasers, differential equations, graph algorithms. His enthusiasm waned early on, as he soon found himself doing very little and horribly bored.

In 2022, to the surprise of a lot of people, tech companies started laying off huge numbers of employees. In a matter of months, hundreds of thousands of tech employees lost their jobs around the world. A dramatic example of that was Twitter, which fired 75% of its workforce. The layoffs continued over the following years.

A recruitment agent told me that he didn't understand how it was even possible to run a company with such a dramatically reduced workforce. He explained to me that when one person from his team went on holiday, the rest struggled to keep up with all the work. To me, there was no mystery there; I had the impression that tech companies had hired too many people and many employees didn't have all that much to do.

In March 2023, I wrote an article in which I said I wasn't surprised about the layoffs and that little would change for those companies. I argued, "After being employed in the tech sector for years, I have come to the conclusion that most people in tech don't work. I don't mean we don't work hard; I mean we almost don't work at all. Nada. Zilch. And when we do get to do some work, it often brings low added value to the company and its customers. All of this while being paid an amount of money some people wouldn't even dream of." While I didn't mean to say that absolutely no one worked in tech—I'd certainly met people who did work, and I'd worked myself at times—I had the impression that the number of idle tech employees had grown enormously.

I didn't write that article expecting anyone to read it; I just thought someone might find it useful someday. But the article went viral, and hundreds of tech employees reached out to me to share their stories of how they weren't working much. Many of them told me this made them extremely unhappy. At first, they were excited to join cutting-edge tech companies and wanted to work hard to build useful products. However, they ended up in overstaffed teams because a manager went on a hiring spree or because they were forced to follow a productivity-killing work methodology. This is not what they'd signed up for.

That same month, stories of idle tech employees started to circulate in the news. An article in *Fortune* revealed that companies like Google and Meta had hired "thousands of people to do 'fake work' to hit hiring metrics out of vanity." An investor commented, "There's nothing for these people to do—it's all fake work. Now that's being exposed. What do these people actually do? They go to meetings."[1]

An article on *Business Insider* reported the story of a Meta employee "paid to not work." The employee explained, "I am one of those employees that was kind of hired into a really strange position where they immediately put me into a group of individuals that was not working. You had to fight to find work. They were hoarding us like Pokémon cards. I could have taken a day off and no one would have known. I think there were probably people who were just checking in and then doing nothing."[2] The employee said she worried about her future career, as she wasn't gaining any experience.

A few months later, another article revealed the story of a research scientist at Amazon who was hired for $300,000 a year but given very little work, and the company concocted a fake project to try to make him happy:

> Within four months of his start at the company, it became clear that Amazon had no idea what to do with him. He spent the next two years bouncing around—switching teams, watching project leaders get promoted despite, he said, producing nothing of substance, and

generally spinning his wheels. Graham was paid more than $300,000 a year but had little work to show for it. Feeling adrift with nothing to do, he gradually disengaged from his job and was eventually put on Amazon's formal performance-management plan.

Facing the threat of firing, Graham was finally put on a project to use machine learning to improve Amazon's music recommendations, which he described as "the first really interesting thing I worked on." He was happy to feel like a valuable member of the team, but Graham's manager told him something stunning: The finished project, which Graham worked on for more than a month, wouldn't see the light of day. It was simply an exercise to satisfy the terms of his performance plan and string out his employment, he was told. Graham left Amazon soon after.[3]

Later that year, *Fortune* shared the testimony of a Google employee who made $150,000 a year and worked less than two hours a day, so he used his free time to build his own business on the side:

> Devon, a pseudonym *Fortune* is using to protect his privacy, begins his week writing code for "a decent part" of any given assignment before sending it off to his manager. That "basically guarantees" him smooth sailing for the rest of the week. He says he typically wakes up around 9 a.m. to shower and make breakfast before working until 11 a.m. or noon, at which point he switches to working on his start-up until 9 or 10 p.m. (Fortune reviewed time-stamped screenshots showing the ex-

tent of start-up work that Devon performed during his workday.) Devon counts himself among the thousands of tech workers who, by their own admission, are paid to do nothing.[4]

The epidemic of tech unproductivity doesn't just affect tech; it affects a lot of people who have little to do with it. One reason for this is that high-paid, idle techies have a lot of free time and money to spend on all sorts of stuff, from soy lattes to houses, which shapes the wider economy. Moreover, if you remember, a lot of the money which funds tech is other people's money, as pension funds, universities, and governments channel money toward venture capital, which then goes to tech. Perhaps some of your savings fund tech's unproductivity.

In this chapter, we'll discuss the causes and mechanics of tech's unproductivity. We first explore why some tech companies go on hiring sprees. We then describe the day-to-day work of techies and explain why a series of trendy "recipes," which are instructions meant to help increase work efficiency and accelerate innovation, may have actually killed productivity and made techies constantly build products only to throw them away soon after. These recipes have been spreading outside the tech sector, so we should all watch out!

## HIRING SPREES

A year ago, a company decided to build a rough prototype of a promising AI-based product in order to assess whether it would satisfy customer needs. Building a prototype was indeed a good idea because it's often hard to know in advance whether an AI-based approach will work well for a certain task, so it's best to test the waters. Somewhere along the way, however, the managers got a little bit too excited, perhaps because everybody was talking about AI at the time. So, instead of waiting until the prototype was finished, they decided to hire ten people to develop and commercialize the full product, including data scientists, data engineers, product managers, and a corporate communications specialist. I asked the team leaders why they didn't finish the prototype first to see whether it worked as expected. They told me this wasn't necessary and explained, "We're confident AI will work well."

This is just one example of a common occurrence in tech: Companies get very excited about trendy technologies, such as AI, blockchain, and augmented reality, and go on hiring sprees. Sometimes they even hire without knowing what exact product the new hires will build. For example, I know a company which hired a team of seventy people to develop an AI-related product before formulating what that product would do or even speaking with prospective users to know their needs. (More on this later.)

In some cases, tech companies hire employees preemptively in anticipation of future growth, which some people call "hiring ahead of demand."[5] For example, I know a start-up which hired employees with niche skills right after receiving funding from a VC, even though they didn't have anything for them to do. They explained to me that they didn't want to waste time trying to find that specialized talent later should the need arise. Companies like Google and Meta have even been accused of hiring people just to remove them from the job market and thus prevent competitors from hiring them.[6] These were some of the luxuries companies could afford during the latest tech boom, when the sector received more money than ever.

In addition, some people may find overstaffing beneficial. For example, the career progression of managers is often measured by how many people they manage, so they might prefer to grow a team even if there isn't enough work for everyone. Start-ups also tend to be taken more seriously when they grow the size of their staff. Moreover, companies that provide technology services to others bill more to their clients the higher the headcount they devote to their projects.

Overstaffing may go more unnoticed in tech than other sectors because businesspeople often don't understand the technical aspects of the work. So, they may believe a task is much harder than it actually is. It would be much harder for, say, a barber, to pretend that cutting someone's hair takes days, as everyone has had a haircut before and roughly understands what a haircut entails, but when it comes to technology, not so many outsiders know the details. In addition, a lot of tech work is abstract and happens behind the scenes—think of a preventative security enhancement—so there isn't always a tangible output that outsiders can relate to.

One of my friends told me that a business manager in his company wanted to outsource a technological task to an external firm and reached out to one of the big consulting companies for a quote. The company proposed devoting a team of several people to the task for a couple of months, and it quoted a few hundred thousand dollars for the job. My friend, who was a techie, told the manager not to proceed and offered to do the job himself. He completed it in two weeks.

While overstaffing may be one of the root causes of idleness, there must be a mechanism that stretches out work, keeping techies busy with unproductive tasks. That's where we go next.

## TASK BLOATING

Up until the 2000s, building software was approached similarly to the construction of bridges and skyscrapers: it was first thoroughly designed, then built, then tested. This became known as the *waterfall* methodology, which referred to the fact that a series of steps were executed in order without looking back.

The waterfall methodology didn't work very well. Compared to bridges and skyscrapers, software is intangible, so it's hard for customers to visualize the end product ahead of time and validate that it satisfies their needs. Moreover, as technology evolves fast, customer needs often change quickly while a product is developed. So, designing the full product in advance and then building it often results in the wrong product. In addition, unlike buildings, software is usually never finished; new features are constantly added to it for years.

Things changed in 2001. A group of dissident software professionals, who advocated steering away from the waterfall methodology, met to discuss the situation and propose an alternative, which they called Agile. One of them explained, "On February 11–13, 2001, at The Lodge at Snowbird ski resort in the Wasatch mountains of Utah, seventeen people met to talk, ski, relax, and try to find common ground—and of course, to eat. What emerged was the Agile Software Development Manifesto."[7]

The manifesto contained a series of values and principles to improve the software development process. These included:

> Our highest priority is to satisfy the customer through early and continuous delivery of valuable software.

Deliver working software frequently, from a couple of weeks to a couple of months, with a preference to the shorter timescale.[8]

In summary, the Agile Manifesto advocated building working software little by little and validating it with the customer along the way. This way, customers provided useful feedback, and it was easy to course-correct if needed.

Agile principles were a valuable addition to the profession. Gone were the days of working for months behind the scenes to deliver the wrong product to the customer. However, things took a dark turn somewhere along the way, as a series of Agile "recipes" became very popular.

Agile recipes were step-by-step instructions which promised to make a team Agile-compliant but at the same time make work more predictable and manageable. These recipes told techies to be flexible and build a product one chunk at a time, just like suggested in the Agile manifesto, but also told them exactly how to plan and organize each chunk and how the day-to-day work should go. This was a dream come true for the management of software projects, as the recipes promised to turn a software team into a "factory" that outputted new stuff at regular intervals. They would also help business managers track progress metrics, make estimates, and identify bottlenecks.

One of the recipes, called *Scrum*, became extremely popular and is now adopted by default across the tech world. Scrum is often imposed from the top across an entire organization. Scrum dictates that work should be organized around small periods of time called *sprints*, which typically last two weeks.

At the beginning of each sprint, team members participate in a long meeting to plan the current sprint's work. They start by analyzing each pending task in a backlog and collectively "size" it, which means to estimate its difficulty, often in terms of the number of days required to complete it.

The most detailed version of Scrum says team members must size tasks by playing a game called *planning poker*. At each round of the game, all participants size one task by casting a secret vote. For this, they must pick a card with a number on it describing the estimated size, and put it face down on the table so others can't see it. The available numbers on the cards belong to a Fibonacci sequence—1, 2, 3, 5, 8, 13, 21, 34, 55 and 89, and so on. I haven't found a consistent explanation for this odd choice of numbers, but one of them is that it discourages spending too much time fine-tuning estimates of harder tasks.

After everyone casts a vote, all cards on the table are flipped at the same time to reveal estimates to others. The task size is chosen by majority vote, but there may be follow-up discussions or voting rounds if some team members pick numbers well above or below those of others. If a task is too large to fit within one single sprint, it is split up into multiple sub-tasks and each of them sized by further rounds of planning poker.

This ritual is sometimes taken very seriously; in fact, the trademark Planning Poker is registered by a software company, which manufactures and sells the official Planning Poker card decks. There are also plenty of browser-based planning poker tools for online meetings. I even worked for a company which developed its own planning poker app for its employees.

After the planning meeting concludes, tasks are distributed among team members based on their preferences. Afterward, team members work on their assigned tasks for the duration of the sprint. According to Scrum, all team members must meet every morning for a short catch-up. During this meeting, participants must share with everyone else what they did the day before, what they plan to work on the present day, and whether there are any blockers. This meeting should be held standing up, which is meant to make people feel uncomfortable so they try to keep it short. Unfortunately, these meetings often last longer than intended, as people end up giving lengthy updates. Some companies have found creative solutions to this problem. For example, I heard of a company that asked participants to do a straining ab workout whenever they spoke during the meeting, such as a forearm plank.

At the end of the sprint, Scrum dictates that team members must meet with stakeholders, such as clients and upper managers, in order to showcase their work and gather feedback. This meeting, called the sprint review, usually lasts at least two hours, as every task must be discussed. In addition, team members must hold a separate, private meeting called a "retrospective" to discuss how the past two weeks went and do self-reflection. After this, the sprint is concluded and the next one starts with a brand-new planning poker game.

The Scrum recipe, although well intentioned, doesn't seem to work quite as expected a lot of the time. The first time I joined a planning poker meeting, I noticed everyone seemed to severely exaggerate their estimated task sizes. For example, one task was to analyze a couple of short code templates found online and see what they could be used for. Anyone familiar with software development would be able to do this in a couple of hours at most.

However, in the poker planning meeting, most of my

colleagues voted that this task required many days of work. I went against the flow, giving it the lowest possible size in the Fibonacci sequence. My colleagues put me in the spotlight, asking me why I thought it was so easy. It was hard to defend my point of view without implying that others were systematically exaggerating their estimates. So, after a few diplomatic exchanges, we ended up slightly adjusting the task size downward. I started to suspect that every task was collectively bloated in the estimates.

In the following sprint, a task was writing a paragraph summarizing the results of a task I'd done myself in the previous sprint. I voted the lowest possible size in the planning poker game, as I thought it was a ten-minute task. However, my colleagues didn't agree; they all voted that my task was worthy of several days of work. While I argued for a bit, I ended up going with the flow, as I didn't want to sound like I was accusing others of a task-bloating conspiracy.

Sometimes, very simple tasks got broken down into many pieces and planned separately. For example, one task was deciding which software tool to use for a certain need. We had a list of required features and four candidate tools, so we had to find out which of the tools covered more of the necessary features. It seemed to me that this could take one person a couple of days if done thoroughly. But the task was broken down into four different subtasks to individually investigate each of the four candidate tools. Each of these four subtasks was assigned many days to complete.

During my time working in Scrum teams, I noticed that bloated tasks were rarely completed before the end of the sprint no matter how easy they were. Instead, they seemed to "expand" over the entire two weeks. This made the daily stand-up meetings rather comical, as people's updates about their work were remarkably thin, but everyone nodded along. This may be an example of Parkinson's Law, which states that "work expands so as to fill the time available for its completion."[9] This principle was formulated in 1955 by naval historian Cyril Northcote Parkinson, who noticed that the number of public sector administrators kept increasing "irrespective of any variation in the amount of work (if any) to be done."

It is tempting to jump to conclusions and determine that task bloating is caused by laziness—techies just want to sit on their beanbags all day. However, that might not be the primary reason.

Task bloating might be a consequence of the imposition of Agile recipes themselves. These recipes try to make each sprint predictable and have the team output something new at the end of each sprint, which may encourage employees to protect themselves by bloating their estimates. This helps them add wiggle room and make sure they can complete their tasks within the sprint and deliver something new each time. So, productivity is sacrificed in the name of predictability.

In addition, task bloating might be a direct result of overstaffing. Suppose a decision-maker gets a bit too excited and decides to hire too many people for a job. The new recruits are enthusiastic at first, but they soon realize there isn't enough work for everyone. So, they become afraid they'll lose their jobs and start pretending to be busier than they are. Managers may look away because downsizing isn't great for their careers either.

## META WORK

Back in 1975, software engineer Fred Brooks wrote an influential book called *The Mythical Man-Month*. The book claimed that splitting tasks among too many software engineers delayed software projects instead of accelerating them. This was because engineers had to spend too much effort talking about their tasks with others to coordinate work.[10] The popular Agile recipes seem to have exacerbated the problem.

Agile recipes make employees spend a lot of time speaking about work instead of working. Every task, even the most menial one, is discussed in the planning meeting. Afterward, the task is discussed again every day during the stand-up meeting. Then it is discussed again during the review meeting at the end of the sprint. So, people speak about each task before doing it, while doing it, and after doing it. These meetings are all instances of "meta-work" rather than actual work. I used to joke that the reason Facebook was renamed "Meta" was that its employees "meta-worked" a lot.

Sometime meta-work takes longer than work itself. I once attended a planning meeting in which attendees discussed for twenty minutes whether a five-minute task should be included in the next sprint or not. Moreover, Scrum makes everyone repeatedly listen to everyone's updates, but tasks are rarely so interconnected that everyone is interested in all of the updates. So, in practice, people often end up getting distracted and playing with their phones when others speak. In addition to being time killers, excessive meetings can also be mood killers; technical work often requires creative problem-solving, and creativity may be curtailed by constantly having to talk about work and give progress updates.

People from other fields are sometimes surprised at how much time we techies spend in meetings. I once asked a partner at a prominent law firm whether he had daily catch-up meetings with the associates. He told me, "No. We're too busy for that. We cannot afford to constantly meet to catch up, as we have important things to do."

I've met a huge number of techies who don't think all that meta-work makes a productive use of their time. So, why don't they just change the recipe? Not so fast!

## THE DOGMA

A few years ago, while I was part of a Scrum team, I suggested that I wasn't sure daily stand-up meetings were the best use of our time. A colleague told me, rather abruptly, "Well, in this company we enjoy teamwork. Don't you?"

Ironically, Agile recipes have been adopted very rigidly. They're often taken at face value and followed to the letter, and they're often imposed as blanket policies without consulting team members or adapting them to the circumstances. They've become a dogma, and those who question them are condemned as heretics.

If you ever suggest an Agile recipe isn't working for you, its proponents will probably tell you it's because you haven't followed it strictly or long enough. For example, someone messaged me the following in response to an article where I expressed my skepticism about Scrum:

> Agile and Scrum are disciplines that need to be mastered and it doesn't happen in a jiffy. ... This reminds me of the race between the tortoise and the hare. The winner had the discipline to stick to the plan of winning the race.

Another person told me:

> So much of what you describe here is indicative of "bad managers," not some inherent flaw with the Agile methodology. Blame the craftsman, not the tools, when the tools are used incorrectly.

As Agile recipes seem so hard to get right, there's been a proliferation of Agile training services, coaches, and certifications. An Agile coach sent me the following message:

> As an Agile Coach, what I read in the article is not agile or any incarnation of Scrum. It is nothing less than bad Agile. And it is a very common occurrence.

One of my friends used to joke, "Agile is like communism; the reason it's never worked is that it's never been applied correctly."

If you dare question an aspect of an Agile recipe, such as the need for daily meetings, its proponents may even suggest that you should somehow be "reeducated" to understand why the recipe is correct. An Agile coach explained to me:

> Scrum ceremonies [i.e., meetings] are a way for the team to interact with themselves and stakeholders. They foster teamwork and transparency. If the meetings are not facilitated properly, or if the team does not understand why these meetings are important, then retraining by the coach or Scrum Master is needed to reiterate the importance of what the team is doing.

I sometimes get the impression that the Agile dogma infantilizes the workforce—techies are told when to meet and what to say. They're also asked to play card games and do ab workouts while they speak. And, if they're naughty, they're scolded by an Agile coach.

In 2019, a *Forbes* article called Agile a religion:

> I knew the end of Agile was coming when we started using hockey sticks. Every morning, at precisely eight o'clock, the team of developers and architects would stand around a room paneled in white boards and would begin passing around a toy hockey stick. When you received the hockey stick, you were supposed to launch into the litany: "Forgive me, Father, for I have sinned. I only wrote two [software] modules yesterday, for it was a day of meetings and fasting." ... The holy hockey stick would then get passed on to the next developer, and like nervous monks, the rest of us would breathe a sigh of relief when we could hand off the damned stick to the next poor schmuck in line. This was no longer a methodology. It had become a religion.[11]

Agile recipes have become so popular that they're spreading outside tech. One of my relatives, who is a graphic designer for a marketing agency, called me a few days ago to catch up. She told me she was a bit frustrated at work because her team had adopted "this methodology" which was making her waste so much time in meetings. She explained to me, with an incredulous tone, that every morning they made her listen to updates from all her colleagues about what they'd done the day before. When she complained about it to her superiors, they told her she had to be a team player.

I asked her, "Does this thing have a name by any chance?"

"Scrum," she replied.

## BRUTE FORCE

In 2022, an upper manager of a top-tier investment bank noticed that AI was turning into the next big thing. He also noticed that the many AI engineers scattered across the organization didn't use a common set of software tools for their work, so they struggled to communicate and share data with one another. So, he thought the company should build its own in-house AI tool, which would be used by all AI engineers. He quickly hired a team of seventy people to build it.

A few months after the project started, the team showed me what they'd been working on so far. They'd built a functional and beautifully designed browser-based tool. But when I looked at it more carefully, I was a bit surprised, as the tool's features seemed to have little to do with how AI engineers usually worked. For example, it let users share their data by uploading Excel files; however, AI engineers rarely used Excel files. As I kept looking at the tool, I found more and more ways in which it didn't seem to relate much to AI work practices.

I thought that, perhaps, the tool targeted AI use cases that were different from what I was used to. So, I asked a team member what type of problems their intended users worked on. She told me they'd never spoken with an intended user. Instead, the team of designers was asked to imagine what a tool to help AI engineers would look like and design it. Afterward, software developers had turned the design into a working product.

I was a bit puzzled, so a manager explained to me that the team sought to build a tool quickly and put it in front of the intended users to collect feedback. He told me that asking hypothetical questions to potential users is unreliable; instead, it's much better to directly give users a real product, have them use it, and collect feedback. In fact, team members were expressively forbidden from speaking with potential users. He added that the team was following a "fail fast" approach.

I thought to myself it was a "fail for sure" approach.

A few months later, I spoke with the founders of a start-up which was trying to innovate in the area of retail management software. The founders picked this field on a hunch, without having ever worked in it and without knowing how they could do anything better or differently from well-established competitors. They told venture capitalists they would use AI to revolutionize the field, but they would have to do experiments to find out how they'd do it. The VCs gave them $100,000 to experiment.

The start-up decided to build a small replica of an existing product, which contained an exact copy of some of its features without doing anything new. I was puzzled about this because it seemed like reinventing the wheel, but they explained to me that they wanted to put this product in front of real users so they could collect feedback. This would help them identify potential areas of improvement.

These two stories of rushing to build products aren't coincidental; they're part of an increasingly popular tech movement which advocates using brute force and trial and error to find a product that resonates with customers. This movement seems to be inspired by a methodology called *lean start-up*, popularized by entrepreneur Eric Ries. In 2008, Ries noticed that the traditional marketing approach didn't work for start-ups. He explained that "a good plan, a solid strategy and thorough market research" don't work "because start-ups operate with too much uncertainty. Startups do not yet know who their customer is or what their product should be."[12] So, he proposed a different approach: take a leap of faith and quickly build a minimum viable product, or MVP, and test it out with real customers as soon as you can. Ries explained:

> The minimum viable product is that product which has just those features (and no more) that allows you to ship a product that resonates with early adopters; some of whom will pay you money or give you feedback.[13]

The MVP lets a start-up quickly obtain tangible feedback from real customers, which is the most valuable kind of feedback. If feedback is good, the start-up continues its direction of work and adds more features to the product. If not, it chooses a new direction of work, which is known as a *pivot*.

While the lean approach was first geared toward start-ups, it soon expanded across the entire tech industry and beyond. Even large companies now build MVPs to test the waters with new products. Entrepreneur Steve Blank said, "The lean start-up changes everything," and described it as an approach that "favors experimentation over elaborate planning, customer feedback over intuition, and iterative design over traditional 'big design up front' development."[14] Mantras like "fail fast" quickly gained popularity, and it was reported that Mark Zuckerberg directed Facebook employees to "Move fast and break things."[15]

I am a big fan of the lean approach and try to implement it in my own work and advise others to do so. When we build products, we always make assumptions about customers, even if we think we know them well. So, we always take a leap of faith. Therefore, it's a good idea to build an MVP quickly and put it in front of customers to validate our assumptions.

Over the years, however, it seems that the leap of faith has become larger and larger, turning the lean approach into a brute-force approach. Instead of trying to understand customers, making sensible assumptions, and building an MVP to validate them, start-ups rush to build *anything* as quickly as possible, just like in the examples we discussed above. According to the brute-force approach, trying to understand customers ahead of time isn't fruitful; instead, you should just build an MVP and collect feedback. If feedback isn't good, don't worry—you can always pivot!

The brute-force approach makes any product seem worth building, even the most outlandish one. I've heard many entrepreneurs and venture capitalists dismiss criticism of farfetched start-up ideas on the grounds that "start-ups are experiments," "you're never sure until you try," and "Airbnb and Netflix only became a success after they pivoted." This may explain why start-ups like Juicero or Quibi received so much support.

Innovation by brute force seems rather wasteful, as it advocates performing expensive experiments to test unlikely hypotheses. Some people think there are more efficient ways of building innovative products. A strategy consultant argues, "Which approach to product innovation makes more sense? You identify the customer's top 20 unmet needs and then conceptualize a solution that addresses them, or you conceptualize a solution you think customers will want and then test/iterate on the solution until it hopefully addresses the customers top unmet needs?"[16]

The proliferation of the brute-force approach has an unpleasant consequence for techies: when they do manage to get some work done, it's often to build products that will never be used except as an experiment before the next pivot. And it's no fun.

The tech-inspired, brute-force approach has been spreading to other sectors. For example, I recently met the managers of a company which sells educational video courses. Instead of researching the market to identify promising topics, the company randomly hires experts on a wide variety of areas, from cooking to English, and has them build "course MVPs," which are short, introductory courses on their respective areas of expertise. They release these courses as quickly as possible, hoping to find profitable topics by accident. Time will tell whether their gains outweigh the cost and pain of doing so many experiments.

## THE MEAT GRINDER

One of my friends, who works for a venture capital firm, is in charge of screening aspiring start-up founders before the firm invests in them. As part of the screening process, he once sent a group of candidates on a trip to Wales, where they had to sleep in tents, hike in the rain, and perform other sporty activities. I was a bit puzzled, so he explained to me that this was meant to assess their resilience—those who couldn't cope with getting their feet wet were not cut out to be founders. He then told me that resilience is one of the most desirable characteristics of founders, as it enables them to endure the successive pivots necessary to build a winning start-up.

Over the past few years, there's been a growing belief that the creation of successful start-ups can be "industrialized," that you just need to follow a process. The first step of the process is putting together a solid founding team—resilient people with compatible skills and interests. Afterward, the founders use the brute-force approach to repeatedly experiment with product ideas and pivot until hitting the jackpot. There's no need for founders to know each other from before or even focus on topics they have experience with.

This process makes me think of a meat grinder of start-ups: You put good founder ingredients in one end and, after cranking and cranking the handle, the ingredients are processed, and start-ups come out the other end. The belief in this process may explain why a company like Mistral received so much funding despite not having a business model—it had a stellar founding team, and the rest isn't so important because it can pivot and pivot.

There's been a proliferation of venture capital firms which try to use the meat grinder approach to create their own start-ups in-house. They often do it in a way that resembles a reality TV show: They put a bunch of people in a room for weeks and ask them to team up, think of start-up ideas, and pitch them to a panel of judges—or be eliminated. The teams that make it all the way to the end receive funding to help them build their MVPs in exchange for shares of their start-ups. People have described these programs as "start-up factories," "*Love Island* for founders," and even "musical chairs on acid."[17]

I participated in one of those programs a couple years ago, which was run by a VC firm every quarter in many cities around the world. I applied online and went through a series of interviews in which they assessed whether I was start-up founder material. I passed the test and was invited to join the program, alongside fifty other people I'd never met. The program lasted three months and required full-time involvement. All participants were paid a modest wage to cover living expenses, and some even had their visas sponsored to move into the country from overseas. It was serious stuff.

The program started on a Monday morning. The organizers explained to us that the most important ingredient to build a successful start-up was having a solid founding team because founders were in for a long ride and couldn't be easily replaced. So, for the next three weeks, they made us participate in various group activities to get to know each other, such as making videos and debating controversial topics. It was quite intense. We were in the same room from 10 a.m. to 7 p.m. every day. By the end of this period, we had to form dream founding teams. Those who hadn't formed a team by then had to leave the program.

The organizers then explained to us that the second-most important ingredient for a successful start-up was finding a promising problem to solve. However, it wasn't as critical as the founding team because it was easier to pivot from problem to problem. Our next job was to find interesting problems that our future start-ups could solve.

Almost none of the participants had joined the program with a specific problem in mind that they wanted to tackle. In fact, this seemed to be discouraged. So, we had to work together to find problems to solve. We were told that one way to do this was to make a list of all the things we did in our daily lives, from the moment we brushed our teeth in the morning to the moment we went to bed in the evening, and identify things that bugged us. We had to try to find a problem that was large enough for a VC to be interested in it. They said a start-up should have the potential to be sold for at least $200 million within seven years, or else it wouldn't be VC material. We had to gather evidence that our problem was as big as that. For example, we could try to obtain letters from potential customers claiming they'd pay a lot to have this problem solved.

Afterward, teams had to present the team and the problem to a jury. Selected teams would receive $100,000 from the VC to build an MVP, in exchange for 10% of the start-up's shares. My team decided not to present anything to the jury—after lengthy discussions, we couldn't find a problem or a way to present it we were confident about. I enjoyed the overall experience because I learned more about start-ups and met people with remarkable backgrounds. However, I was skeptical of the approach. It seemed too easy: Just put founder ingredients in a room for long enough and successful start-ups will be launched.

The meat grinder approach has created a huge number of new start-ups. One VC firm, for example, launched over a thousand start-ups using this sort of reality TV approach, and another one launched over five hundred.[18]

So far, the results of this approach don't seem very impressive. Technology reporter Amy Lewin noted that few of the start-ups launched by these programs are successful. She argues that this "undermines the thesis that if you bring amazing talent together, they can build great companies."[19] Most start-ups I know of which started this way ended up going out of business within a year. A venture capitalist told me these programs rarely work well because they confuse *necessary* with *sufficient*—a resilient founding team and a promising problem to solve are necessary but not enough to launch a successful start-up.

## MISERY

When I told friends I was bored at work, some of them made fun of me—why did I complain about being paid a lot to do very little? One of them told me I reminded him of Meghan Markle and Prince Harry. But after speaking with many idle tech employees, I noticed the situation made most of them miserable. They didn't join this field to sit on a beanbag all day; they joined it because they wanted to build cool stuff that would be used by others one day. In addition, some people told me that putting on a show to pretend to work was soul-crushing and more taxing than working. Moreover, not working put their careers on hold because they didn't learn new skills, which is particularly important in the fast-moving technology sector. An idle Meta employee said, "This kind of experience gets me nowhere. I don't have metrics I can put on my résumé."[20]

Some people have become worried the epidemic of idleness could cause social grievance. A former idle employee argues, "There must be resentment building up. People who are self-employed and who work hard, in trades, and who are not part of this gravy train, see the middle classes having this very nice and comfortable life. They see a new leisure class that says it works but doesn't. What should they think?"[21] This is rather unfortunate, as many techies aren't trying to be idle but struggle to find useful work to do.

Things don't get much better for the techies who do work, as many of them, due to the brute-force approach to innovation, spend their office hours building stuff that nobody will ever use, and they know it. I know many techies who became disengaged from work when they realized what they were building would only be used as part of a crazy experiment and then dumped.

The lack of opportunities to do useful work has made

some techies reconsider their careers. A software developer sent me the following message:

> I'm 37 years old and have spent nearly 15 years working in jobs where I could have completed tasks much more efficiently. I'm tired of attending endless Zoom calls where "managers" spout nonsense, and everything is "Agile," translating to more time spent tracking tasks than actually doing them. I've billed countless hours to our client [a famous retail brand] while watching TV shows, YouTube videos, or reading novels, waiting for those "Agile" managers to give me direction. Despite being considered a "rockstar" in software development, I feel empty.
>
> I recently stumbled upon one of your articles while reflecting on my life choices. A fellow developer shared it with me, and I can't express how much your words resonated with me over the past week. Your article reassured me that I'm not alone or crazy for wanting to live off my savings and switch careers entirely.
>
> Warmest regards,
> Alex

A few weeks after sending me this message, Alex quit his career as a corporate software developer and moved back to his hometown to live cheaply off his savings and figure out what to do next. He then decided to start his own business—a niche app which he intends to commercialize soon. He told me he's finally managed to put his skills to good use and remembered how much he likes to code. He also said he hadn't been this busy in a very long time.

# CHAPTER 6:

# WHAT WE CAN DO

Over the past few years, the tech sector has gone a little crazy. In the following, I'll share my thoughts on how we could make things better. We'll go back to each of the chapters of this book, which described a different aspect of the tech craze, and I'll share how I think we could turn that craze around. I hope you'll find some of my suggestions helpful even if you're not part of the tech industry. Let's go!

## CHAPTER 1: FROM MIRACULOUS TO BORINGLY USEFUL

Gatwick is a major airport near London which handles a whopping eight hundred flights a day. The airport is tightly packed and can only use one runway at a time, so minor inconveniences can cause severe delays. Until 2019, Gatwick had no way to track the location of most ground vehicles around the airport. For example, it was impossible for people in the control room to know the location of baggage carts, boarding stairs, and firetrucks. This often caused serious problems.

For instance, boarding stairs would sometimes be mistakenly left blocking a service road, which resulted in accidents and delays.

A medical company, which built defibrillators and technology for ambulances, came across this problem when researching Gatwick's operations. The company made a proposal to Gatwick to solve the issue: it would install GPS devices in vehicles around the airport, and it would write a piece of software to let people in the control room visualize their locations on a map. In addition, the software would let users configure alerts to inform the control room of potential problems, such as a vehicle stopping on a service road for too long or a vehicle driving too fast. Gatwick accepted the proposal, and the medical company soon deployed its solution to over twelve hundred vehicles. After the successful Gatwick project, the company soon discovered that many other airports were equally incapable of tracking ground vehicles.

When I first heard this story, I was quite surprised—how was it possible that, in 2019, when everyone was speaking about blockchain and artificial intelligence, one of Europe's busiest airports didn't know where its baggage carts were? I started researching the aviation sector and heard many similar stories. For example, I discovered that many airports still logged the movements of fire trucks in and out of fire stations by using paper forms, and a start-up had recently launched a product to help airports digitalize those logs.

I also discovered that aircraft maintenance records are, as of today, kept on paper. Whenever a plane goes through a check-up, a technician fills in the details in a paper form. When a plane switches hands from one airline to another—most airlines rent planes instead of owning them—the owner of the plane must verify that the previous airline complied with all its maintenance duties. This verification process is done manually; someone revises all the paperwork by hand, sheet by sheet. Forms are widely different across countries, which makes this process really cumbersome. I heard of a start-up which tried to automate this process using artificial intelligence, but a user told me the product didn't work well, so he reverted to doing things by hand. The problem remains unsolved.

I've observed equally inefficient processes in many other industries. For example, I recently discovered that retail brands, such as cosmetics, receive weekly sales records by email from each department store where they place their products, say, Harrods, Sephora, and Macy's. Each store sends reports in its own format. For example, Harrods sends a PDF file detailing sales by city, while Sephora sends an Excel file detailing sales by store. So, each week, an employee of the brand has to go through all the files and manually collate the information into one spreadsheet. And there's no easy way to analyze the data afterward. The process is so cumbersome that sometimes brands realize too late their products aren't selling well, and they get kicked out of a department store before being able to take action to correct it.

I used to think we live in a technologically advanced world. However, over the past few years, stories like the above have made me realize many industries are extremely inefficient and could improve their efficiency with technology.

But few people seem to focus on these problems. Instead, as discussed in Chapter 1, many entrepreneurs and investors focus on epic businesses that require a miracle to succeed—the Juiceros and Quibis of the world. These businesses often bet on exciting new technology, such as blockchain, artificial intelligence, and augmented reality. For example, an entrepreneur recently reached out to me to share his revolutionary start-up idea—he wanted to build a product that would use artificial intelligence to try to guess what your pet was trying to tell you and translate it into human language. These ideas sound big but rarely work out very well.

I think techies and businesspeople should focus more energy on solving "boring" problems like the ones described above, which would help old-fashioned industries become more efficient. One of the reasons for it is that solving boring problems is often a good way to create a surprisingly solid business. For example, I've met entrepreneurs who decided to tackle a boring problem and had a queue of clients that signed up to buy the product before it was even built. This was because the product solved a real pain point that customers were desperate to alleviate. This removed much of the uncertainty of launching a business.

Finding a promising boring problem to solve isn't easy; in general, it requires knowing an industry deep enough to identify something missing in it—something which others have overlooked. This goes against the advice given to many aspiring entrepreneurs, who are often told stories of outsiders who revolutionized entire industries and became billionaires. For example, they're told the founders of Airbnb and Uber weren't experts in hospitality or mobility. However, while I haven't met many unicorn billionaires, I've met many millionaires, and most of them made their millions by solving a boring problem in an industry they knew well.

Another reason for solving boring problems is that it's useful and purposeful. This makes boring problems not so boring after all, as it can be quite exciting to build stuff that others use, perhaps more so than building a trendy product that nobody does.

If you still decide to build the epic kind of start-up, I suggest you try not to rely too much on a miracle. For example, instead of hoping to solve a technical problem nobody has solved before, perhaps you can rethink the product so it would still add value to your customers while having a lower technical challenge to overcome. Or you could do some research on possible ways of solving the technical problem before going all in and promising the world to your customers and investors.

## CHAPTER 2: FROM BIG TO SMALL

I know a start-up which was struggling to come up with a product idea that resonated with customers; the company kept creating products within its field of interest and testing them with potential customers, but the response to them was lukewarm.

At one point, thanks to many conversations with people in its target domain, the start-up finally discovered an unsolved problem that many seemed to truly struggle with. However, the start-up projected that, while customers would pay to have that problem solved, they wouldn't pay all that much. So, the start-up would generate a few million a year in revenue instead of the tens or even hundreds of millions it had promised to investors. As a result, the start-up passed on the opportunity and kept looking for a bigger problem. Last time I heard, it was still looking.

In Chapter 2, we discussed that start-ups often aim for big, and they operate at a loss for years in order to fund their explosive growth. My suggestion is that we shouldn't dismiss small businesses so quickly. We should remember that the ultimate goal of a business is to become profitable because that's how it pays its bills and stays afloat in the long run. Sometimes smaller businesses, which solve a pressing problem in a niche market, become profitable really quickly.

In fact, if your goal is to become rich, you may be better off building a small, profitable business than trying to grow a unicorn. When you grow a start-up at a loss, you do so by selling a part of your company to investors. As a result, when the business generates a reward for its owners one day, you must share the pie with others. So, you have to make sure you grow your business large enough that the pie is big and you can reap a good financial reward from your piece. Moreover, investors usually require a money-back guarantee, so if the pie ends up being too small, you may have to give it all up and end up empty-handed.

In addition, when you build a small business, you're more likely to retain control of it. For example, you can decide to pay yourself some money from its profits—in the form of dividends—which is usually expressly forbidden by external investors, who want you to reinvest every penny into growth.

Moreover, targeting a small market can be an advantage in itself—some markets are too small to support multiple profitable competitors, which may deter copycats from entering the market. This could provide a natural moat that protects your profits in the long term.

If you still decide to aim for big, make sure this is a conscious decision driven by an expectation of future profitability—you expect future gains to dwarf the accumulated losses of the growth phase. This is typically reserved to businesses that can develop strong network effects or switching costs, like LinkedIn or Apple, which keep customers captive and stave off competitors. But this doesn't happen as often as it seems.

I even dare say that tech investors themselves could benefit from investing in smaller tech business. The idea of making eyewatering profits from unicorns is seductive, but the numbers show that it doesn't seem to be working very well overall. Perhaps investors would make better returns in the long run from boring, small businesses than from trying to hit the unicorn jackpot.

## CHAPTER 3: FROM VENTURE CAPITAL TO BOOTSTRAPPING

In 2001, a designer teamed up with a DJ-turned-coder to launch a modest web design agency called Rocket Science Group. As the pair worked with clients, they noticed the lack of a simple, cost-effective tool for email marketing automation. So, they decided to build their own to use with their clients. They called it Mailchimp. The founders didn't raise any external funding to build this tool; instead, they used their own savings and income from agency work.

In 2007, the two founders decided to drop their agency work and focus on selling their email marketing software to others, as this seemed like a promising direction of work. The product became profitable quickly and the company self-funded its growth from then on; it never accepted external investment. Over the years, Mailchimp grew to become the world's foremost email automation platform. A decade later, the company was sold to a financial software giant for a whopping $12 billion. The founders, who hadn't split the pie with VCs, made billions in cash from the deal.

When aspiring entrepreneurs come up with a business idea, their instinctive response tends to be to try to raise money from others immediately, especially from venture capitalists—how else are they supposed to kick-start a business?

While VC funding may help founders launch and grow a start-up, it comes with strings. For starters, fundraising itself takes a lot of time, as the different parties must negotiate complicated terms and spend weeks or even months talking to lawyers. I know a start-up that went through months of negotiations to agree the terms of a deal with a group of VCs. After everyone agreed, one VC tried to change the terms of the deal at the last minute. The founders had to reopen negotiations and spend a few bitter weeks speaking with lawyers and investors all over again. The start-up didn't even have a paid customer yet.

Once fundraising is concluded, the story isn't over; you still have to meet VCs regularly and discuss the start-up's direction with them. You're also expected to soon start working toward securing the next fundraising round. Sometimes, I have the impression that founders end up working more for their investors than their customers.

In addition, when VCs invest in a start-up, they usually gain control over important business decisions. For example, the VC can usually prevent the start-up from being sold if the deal isn't deemed good enough. Some VCs even make founders seek their approval before hiring any new senior employee.

Founders lose so much control of their businesses that VCs often kick them out of their management duties altogether, and this happens quite a lot. Business professor Noam Wasserman explained:

> When I analyzed 212 American start-ups that sprang up in the late 1990s and early 2000s, I discovered that most founders surrendered management control long before their companies went public. By the time the ventures were three years old, 50% of founders were no longer the CEO; in year four, only 40% were still in the corner office; and fewer than 25% led their companies' initial public offerings.... Four out of five entrepreneurs, my research shows, are forced to step down from the CEO's post. Most are shocked when investors insist that they relinquish control, and they're pushed out of office in ways they don't like and well before they want to abdicate.[1]

In many cases, founders are kicked out even though their start-ups are doing well. I asked a former VC why this happened, and he told me founders were kicked out *precisely* because their companies were doing well; according to him, VCs seek to gain more control over a company once they think they can make a sizable gain from it.

My advice to start-ups is that they should avoid raising money from others unless it's absolutely necessary. In start-up circles, the practice of building a start-up without external funding is known as *bootstrapping*. Mailchimp is probably the most successful example of a bootstrapped start-up.

Bootstrapping isn't publicized very often. The Mailchimp story, for example, went surprisingly under the radar. A start-up advisor complained, "You'd think there would be gushing stories and endless positive headlines about growing a business without outside funding. A rare unicorn of a big company that didn't raise outside capital. But no. Almost no encouragement for tech companies to grow with customer funding. No VC funding = few stories."[2]

If you're an aspiring founder, try to bootstrap your business as much as possible, perhaps using your own savings or your income from another job. This may sound difficult, but if your business solves a real problem—perhaps the "boring" kind—you may be able to find customers that are willing to pay for your product early on. This could generate enough cashflow to self-fund your operations and even your growth.

A year ago, I met an aerospace engineer who launched a start-up to help satellite manufacturers better coordinate their ground logistics. The business was completely bootstrapped. The first version of the product was very simple, but the problem it solved was so painful for customers that they bought it right away. Moreover, the founder knew the field well, so he could easily approach prospective customers through his well-established network.

After launching the product, the founder started speaking with venture capitalists to raise funding, as this seemed the normal thing to do. When the fundraising agreement with VCs was almost finalized, he decided to cancel fundraising altogether because he realized he didn't need the money—the business was already profitable, and there was enough money to self-fund its growth. Perhaps an injection of money from venture capital would have made expansion faster, but the founder understood this meant losing ownership and control of the company.

If you still decide to raise money from VCs, instead of selling them shares, you may consider an alternative agreement.

For example, a new type of agreement called SAFE has become popular in some circles. Under a SAFE deal, a start-up receives funding in exchange for a promise to give shares to the VC later on instead of releasing them right away. This helps founders retain control of their companies for longer. A new type of agreement called SAFER was introduced in 2023.[3] Similarly to SAFE, under a SAFER agreement the start-up promises to give shares to the VC later on. However, if revenue allows it, the start-up pays interest to VCs over time in exchange for buying back some of the promised shares. So, as the start-up grows, the VC makes a return on its investment and, at the same time, the start-up founders face a lower risk of losing control of their companies.

You may also consider raising funding from angel investors instead of venture capitalists. Angel investors are wealthy individuals who invest their own money into your company. As far as I've heard, they sometimes show signs of having more skin in the game than VCs. For example, they may work more actively to help you find customers and make important decisions.

While there's a place for both raising and not raising VC funding, it seems many entrepreneurs do so because it's the default option or even because it gives them a seal of approval. I think they should make sure they understand that VC funding is not the only way to build a business and that it comes with strings.

I sometimes wonder whether some things could also change within venture capital itself so that it better serves entrepreneurs and those who put their money into VC funds (the "LPs"). For quite some time, people have been arguing that VCs' incentives are misaligned with the goals of entrepreneurs and LPs, especially due to the 2% management fee they charge every year regardless of performance. So, a potential solution may be to change the compensation structure. A group of investors argued, "A better option than the 2% flat management fee is a budget-based management fee based on VC firm operating expenses. The budget-based fee offers better alignment."[4]

They also argued for more transparency into how VC firms compensate their managers and an improved way of calculating performance metrics. In addition, they suggested that evergreen funds, which don't have an end date and can keep reinvesting their gains, could be a better choice than the current setup: "Evergreen funds are open-ended and therefore not subject to the fixed timeframe of a ten-year fund life or the pressure and distraction of fundraising every four to five years." Alternatively, a venture capitalist suggested that a potential antidote to misalignment would be for VC firms to actively shift away from investing other people's money and start investing their own.[5]

But I'm not sure things will change, as the current setup seems to work well for VCs and has remained stable for years. I recently spoke with a venture capitalist who told me he thought the industry was broken and the 2% fee was a major source of misalignment. He was about to launch his own VC firm at the time, so I asked him how he intended to structure the firm's compensation. He said he would still do it the usual way, with the infamous 2% management fee. I asked him whether he thought that was weird given what he'd just told me. He answered he didn't think it was weird because, compared to other VCs, he would *really* work in the best interests of his entrepreneurs and LPs, so he would truly earn the management fee.

## CHAPTER 4: FROM QUICK FIX TO BIG PICTURE

In dire economic times, policymakers and economists try to help; they come up with new economic theories and policy prescriptions to navigate the slump and restore prosperity. For example, in the midst of the 1930s' depression, economist John Maynard Keynes suggested that the government should spend a lot of money to compensate for the private sector's lack of spending; this would help decrease unemployment and recover from the crisis. He argued that if the government didn't find useful things to spend on, it was still worth spending on unnecessary projects like building monuments, as this would create jobs.[6]

Keynes took his suggested policy even further and argued:

> If the Treasury were to fill old bottles with banknotes, bury them at suitable depths in disused coalmines which are then filled to the surface with town rubbish, and leave it to private enterprise on well-tried principles of laissez-faire to dig the notes up again ... there need be no more unemployment and, with the help of the repercussions, the real income of the community, and its capital wealth also, would probably become a good deal greater than it actually is. It would, indeed, be more sensible to build houses and the like; but if there are political and practical difficulties in the way of this, the above would be better than nothing.[7]

Keynes also proposed a recipe to prevent slumps altogether: push interest rates down to zero. He argued this would have the effect of "abolishing slumps and thus keeping us permanently in a quasi-boom."[8]

Perhaps the measures suggested by Keynes would be an effective way to fix the problem at hand. However, whenever we analyze a policy, we must wonder whether it may come with unintended side effects that would negatively affect the economy in the longer term. For example, suppose a government decides to build monuments in an effort to reduce unemployment. What if this increases the going wages of builders and the cost of raw materials? That would make it more expensive for the private sector to complete other, perhaps more useful building projects. Would the government be capable, in practice, to only hire unemployed workers and buy unwanted material, so that the wider building industry isn't impacted by monument building?

We should also think of the potential unintended effects of a zero-interest rate policy. For example, what if it makes entrepreneurs a bit too excited and thus launch nonsensical projects? And what if they borrow too much money, which they can't realistically pay back?

Since the 2008 crisis, as discussed in Chapter 4, governments around the world implemented a package of measures to encourage risk-taking and entrepreneurship, hoping this would dampen the effects of the economic crisis. This particularly impacted the tech sector, and tech investment grew higher than ever. Governments also provided grants to tech entrepreneurs, which they didn't have to pay back, in order to help them pursue innovative projects.

On the surface, these policies seem to help entrepreneurs. However, I think we should analyze policies more holistically than that. We have to wonder, "We can help entrepreneurs, but at what cost?"

For that, we should ask ourselves whether these policies

have unintended consequences. For example, what if they cause bubbles? Are the benefits of a bubble worth the ensuing slump? Does cheap and free money make some entrepreneurs less careful with their budgets? I have met entrepreneurs who, once they received funding, started spending money on unnecessary business trips, hired assistants without really needing them, and explored unpromising product ideas just because they had spare cash. Are those splurges worth it?

In addition to considering the unintended effects of a policy, we must also consider its *opportunity cost*, which is the cost of *not* pursuing an alternative course of action. For example, what if Juicero and Quibi had *not* been created? What would all their engineers have done? Would they have been unemployed? Or would they have worked on other projects, perhaps more useful ones which created longer-lasting value and even economic growth? And what if the government did *not* give so much free money to start-ups? How many of these start-ups would still be able to obtain the money privately, thus not making the taxpayer foot the bill?

It is hard to argue against policies that help tech entrepreneurs—who wants to be the one to say someone should receive less help? But if we keep trying to help without thinking about the unintended consequences and opportunity cost of our help, we risk helping much less than we think.

## CHAPTER 5: FROM RECIPE-DRIVEN TO CUSTOMER-DRIVEN

As the Amazon marketplace grew, its warehouses became larger and busier. So, the company started researching innovative technologies to help track the movement of packages and workers inside its facilities, hoping to improve their operations. For example, in 2015, the company filed a patent describing the use of smart shelves with weight sensors which helped detect when an item was removed from or added to a shelf.[9] And in 2016, Amazon filed another patent describing the use of ultrasonic signals to track the positions of workers' hands in a warehouse.[10]

After so much effort inventing fancy warehouse technology, Amazon wondered what else it could do with it. And the company came up with a fascinating idea: What if it could create high-tech supermarkets where you didn't have to check out at all? Instead, you would identify yourself using an app when entering the store and cameras would monitor your movements as you shopped. After leaving the store, artificial intelligence software would process the footage and send you the bill for your groceries. A promotional video claimed, "What if we could weave the most advanced machine learning, computer vision, and AI into the very fabric of a store so you never had to wait in line?"[11]

In December 2016, Amazon created a prototype of this technology, called Just Walk Out, and trialed it in a Seattle supermarket only open to Amazon employees. The company said it would open the shop to the public in early 2017,[12] although its opening was delayed due to a technological malfunction.[13]

A year later, the shop finally opened and was named Amazon Go. An article in *Bloomberg* revealed that Amazon hoped to open another three thousand similar shops by 2021.[14]

The reception of the shops by the public was lukewarm. It appeared that people didn't care as much about fancy checkout technology as they cared about finding the best shopping deals. A business consultant explained, "Retailers must also provide competitive pricing and an enjoyable customer experience. Just Walk Out isn't enough," to which a strategy consultant added, "Customers are prioritizing to save money. Even the most advanced self-checkout technology won't revert this trend in the short term... It seems Amazon has come to realize this too."[15]

In addition, Amazon Go shops didn't seem cheaper to run than a regular supermarket with self-checkout counters, as they still had to employ people to replenish shelves and even assist shoppers with issues scanning their apps at the door. Moreover, the AI technology never worked well, so around 70% of the transactions had to be reviewed by human workers who watched the videos remotely.[16]

Over the next four years, Amazon opened a few dozen shops equipped with its Just Walk Out technology around the U.S. and the U.K. As the shops weren't as commercially successful as expected, the company soon started closing some of them. In January 2023, it closed one of its shops in London, just sixteen months after it opened. Two months later, it closed eight of its shops in the U.S. Three months later, another three of the London shops closed down.

By early 2024, Amazon only had 42 shops with its Just Walk Out technology. Amazon had also been trying to sell this technology to other supermarkets, but only 130 had bought it across the world.[17] In April 2024, the company announced it would decommission the Just Walk Out technology from some of its shops and stop rolling it out in new ones. A spokesperson acknowledged, "We've heard from customers that while they enjoyed the benefit of skipping the checkout line with Just Walk Out, they also wanted the ability to easily find nearby products and deals, view their receipt as they shop, and know how much money they saved while shopping throughout the store."[18]

I always struggled to understand what problem Amazon was trying to solve for shoppers. Were shoppers really that annoyed about checkouts that they'd flock to Amazon Go shops just to avoid it? Where I live, by the time Amazon Go was launched, most supermarkets had installed numerous self-checkout machines, which had eliminated queues. So, Amazon Go only saved you the time spent scanning items at the machine. Was that such a big problem for customers?

If it was about reducing the cost of operating a supermarket and thus offer better deals, it was also unclear how the technology would accomplish that, as supermarkets with the Just Walk Out technology required as many employees to run as regular supermarkets with self-checkout machines, plus the cost of installing and running the complicated technology.

Over the past few years, I've had the impression that the tech sector has forgotten about customers. I think this may be one of the root causes of the epidemic of tech unproductivity discussed in Chapter 5. For example, instead of prioritizing delivering useful stuff to customers, tech companies prioritize predictability above everything else, so they've adopted stringent work recipes which micromanage work and make techies stretch out their tasks. In addition, instead of trying to genuinely understand customers, many of them follow a brute-force recipe that promises they'll understand them through trial and error.

My suggestion to increase tech productivity is to put customers first, above recipes. We should remember that it is customers we work for.

One way to focus on customers is to embrace Agile principles (not recipes), which tell us we should build a product little by little, validating it with customers along the way. Over the last couple of years, for example, I've taken on software projects as a freelancer, and I've noticed clients tend to dream really big—they want to build a huge product in one go. So, I often ask them to slow down and help them split their product ideas into much more manageable bits. Afterward, we work together to pick the bit that would provide the most satisfaction for the least effort. This way, they can soon experiment with a tangible product and give me feedback. It also motivates me, as I feel I build a relevant feature from the get-go.

I suggest we adopt Agile principles in a more customer-driven way instead of a recipe-driven way. For example, we can ask ourselves, "What is something useful that we could build quickly?" instead of "What can we build that fits within a two-week sprint?" And if we want to measure progress, we can ask, "How many useful features have we delivered to the customer?" instead of "How many items have we cleared from the Scrum backlog?"

When I suggest to others that we don't necessarily have to follow an Agile recipe, some people freak out. They tell me, "But how will you manage day-to-day work?" Indeed, sometimes it is necessary to have a structure in place to organize work or else it becomes chaotic, especially with larger teams. My advice is that such a structure should be decided on a case-by-case basis with the primary goal of better serving customers. In addition, people who do the day-to-day work, such as coders, should have a say in choosing the structure instead of having a recipe imposed on them from above. Some companies already do this to a certain extent; Spotify, for example, gives each team flexibility to pick a recipe or invent one.[19]

A few years ago, I worked for a tech company that built software for travelers. Our team was in charge of building a new piece of software that, once released, would be used by millions of travelers every day. It was the kind of thing that runs behind the scenes so not a lot of people are aware of it, but if it breaks, it can create major complications. For example, the rumor was that, a couple of years before, a team in this company had unknowingly released a broken piece of software, and the business had lost $150,000 every hour until it was fixed. We did not want to do that.

When the day came, we released our software little by little over the course of weeks to make sure it didn't cause disruptions. During those critical weeks, we decided to meet every morning to look together at the data and analyze it to make sure everything was fine. Compared to a "daily stand-up" imposed by a Scrum recipe, we decided ourselves that we needed to meet every day—we really wanted to make sure we didn't break anything. Once the system was fully rolled out, we stopped meeting every day as it was no longer deemed necessary.

Another time, I joined a start-up on a temporary project to help it build a new feature for its app. I built it by myself, as it was a niche thing I had experience with, and then we had to integrate it with the rest of the app. This integration process required back-and-forth communication with the other engineers. We wanted to finish this as fast as we could because customers were expecting the feature, so we decided not to plan the work around sprints or even schedule any meetings. Instead, we decided to work as quickly as possible and have impromptu meetings whenever we needed them just by picking up the phone.

In these two stories, the structure we adopted to organize work was very different—daily meetings versus freestyle—but they had one thing in common: We selected the structure that worked best in the specific situation with the goal of serving our customers.

If you ever decide to adopt a certain recipe but then notice people don't follow it—for example, they don't pay attention in meetings or complain about them—the problem is probably the recipe, not the techies. So, make sure to hear their concerns. If you impose the recipe regardless, you infantilize techies—you tell them to do things against their instincts because you think you know better than them. *Clean your room, or else no TV today!*

My advice regarding the lean approach to innovation—and its exaggerated "brute-force" derivative—is similar: Let's shift toward a more customer-centric approach. Instead of performing random experiments to find something that sticks, we should try to understand our customers first in order to pick experiments that are worth doing. The results of these experiments will let us understand our customers even better and validate our assumptions about them. A business consultant argued:

> When companies get innovation wrong, it's often because they jump right into building solutions. They don't start by studying problem space. The process works far better when you take the time to start in problem space—to understand where people struggle to get a

job done; to decide what unmet outcomes to address; to ensure a solution could emerge that gets the job done significantly better. Once you're armed with that knowledge, you'll be equipped to build something your customers will love.[20]

When companies prioritize delivering great things to customers over following recipes, something magical happens: Customers are happy because their problems are solved and, at the same time, techies are happy because they use their time productively and they build genuinely useful stuff. That's what tech should be about.

# FINAL THOUGHTS

When I was a child, I was fascinated by all types of machines. But there was one that beat them all: elevators. I was intrigued by the mechanisms that moved them up and down a building and opened and closed their doors automatically. As I lived in a rather small town, however, I didn't have many chances to ride an elevator. So, whenever we went on a trip with my parents, I got really excited—it meant we'd stay in a hotel, and hotels often had elevators!

When I was five, we went on a road trip and stayed one night in a hotel that didn't have an elevator. I threw a horrible tantrum, with tears and all. At our next destination, luckily, the hotel had an elevator. One afternoon, I snuck out of the room when my parents weren't looking to ride it by myself. I didn't close the door properly—many were manual back then—so the door moved, and the elevator stopped in between two floors. Without knowing why it'd stopped, I cried for help until I was rescued.

A couple of years later, I discovered something life-changing: there was this shopping mall in a larger city near my hometown that had an elevator with a glass ceiling, so I could look up to see the cables and even the little engine that opened and closed the doors. So, whenever we traveled there, my parents brought me to that mall so I could ride the elevator up and down—I could be entertained rather cheaply.

Over the next few years, my enthusiasm for elevators waned, but others popped up. For example, at one point I became fascinated by barcodes. So, as my parents did their grocery shopping, I navigated the supermarket trying to learn how to guess the numbers that a barcode represented just by looking at it.

At the age of sixteen, I became obsessed with airplanes. I wanted to understand how they worked and how they managed to fly. As it turned out, most of the popular explanations about flight dynamics were incorrect. I then found a life-saving essay called "See How It Flies" which debunked popular explanations and provided a better one.[1]

A couple of years later, I took a flight on a family holiday and sat close to a person who turned out to be a retired physics teacher. He noticed I was looking at the wings through the window, so he thought he could kill time by teaching this teenager a thing or two about airplanes. He told me, "Did you know the usual explanation of how planes fly is not correct? It has little to do with the shape of the wing, as most people think. There's another explanation. You know how water bends around a spoon? I don't remember the name of that phenomenon, but…"

I interrupted him and said, "Are you talking about the Coanda effect?" I then told him that the Coanda effect wasn't a good explanation of why planes flew either and referred him to "See How It Flies." It may have been the most smarty-pants thing I've ever said. I promised I've learned how to behave much better since then.

Naturally, when I grew up, I wanted to be a guy who built stuff—it would allow me to turn all that enthusiasm about science and technology into a career. So, I decided to study computer science at my local university and hoped I'd soon be building things that would be used by thousands of people.

But when I started working in tech, I was shocked. I realized that finding useful work to do in the field was actually pretty hard. Who would have thought? My childhood dreams were crushed.

But it doesn't have to be this way. I hope this book will help raise some awareness about the tech craze, and I hope things will get better in the future for us techies who want to build real stuff.

# ACKNOWLEDGMENTS

I find writing a book much more difficult than it initially seems. The most challenging task is not punctuation or grammar; instead, it is knowing how your audience will respond to your writing. I often wonder, "Is it interesting?" "Is it boring?" "Is it obvious?" "Is it too opinionated?" "Does it go too fast?" "Does it go too slowly?" (By the way, AI can't help much with any of this.)

Sometimes it's very hard to answer those questions unless other people read your draft and share their thoughts. That's why my biggest thank you goes to my beta readers, Adam, Charlotte, and Jesse, who voluntarily read the book as I wrote it, one chapter at a time, and shared valuable feedback to help me improve the manuscript and course-correct when needed.

I'm also grateful to the many people who participated in interviews, shared their stories, and recommended research material.

Finally, I'd like to thank everyone who helped me produce the book. A special shout-out goes out to cover designer Paul Hawkins as well friends and family who helped me pick the book's title (not easy). Without you, the book wouldn't read or look the way it does.

Thank you all!

# NOTES

## INTRODUCTION

1. Weil, Cortney. "Twitter 'Day in a Life' Video Indicates Lots of Downtime, Very Little Actual Work." *Blaze Media*, 27 Oct. 2022, https://www.theblaze.com/news/twitter-day-in-life-video. Accessed 28 Apr. 2024.

2. McArdle, Megan. "Just When You Thought Musk's Twitter Foray Couldn't Get Wilder." *Washington Post*, 23 Oct. 2022, https://washingtonpost.com/opinions/2022/10/23/elon-musk-plans-twitter-job-cuts/. Accessed 28 Apr. 2024.

3. McArdle, Megan. "How Elon Musk Fired Twitter Staff and Broke Nothing." *Washington Post*, 19 Feb. 2023, https://www.washingtonpost.com/opinions/2023/02/19/elon-musk-twitter-layoffs-tech/. Accessed Apr. 2024.

## CHAPTER 1: MIRACLES

1. McCullough, Brian. "An Eye-Opening Look at the Dot-Com Bubble of 2000 — and How It Shapes Our Lives Today." Ideas.ted.com, 4 Dec. 2018, https://ideas.ted.com/an-eye-opening-look-at-the-dot-com-bubble-of-2000-and-how-it-shapes-our-lives-today/. Accessed 28 Apr. 2024.

2. Teare, Gené. "Global Funding Slide in 2022 Sets Stage for Another Tough Year." *Crunchbase News*, 5 Jan. 2023, https://news.crunchbase.com/venture/global-vc-funding-slide-q4-2022/. Accessed 28 Apr. 2024.

3. "Unicorns Guide." *Dealroom.co*, dealroom.co/guides/guide-to-unicorns. Accessed 28 Apr. 2024.

4. Wijngaarde, Yoram. "Global Venture Capital Is Crushing All Records in 2021." *Dealroom.co*, 7 July 2021, https://dealroom.co/blog/global-venture-capital-is-crushing-records-in-h1-2021. Accessed 28 Apr. 2024.

5. Pringle, Eleanor. "'Penned' Tech Specialists Are Earning Six-Figure Salaries to 'Do Nothing' and String out 10-Minute

Tasks." *Fortune*, 7 Apr. 2023, https://fortune.com/2023/04/07/tech-bank-jobs-paid-to-do-no-work. Accessed 28 Apr. 2024.

6   Gompers, Paul, et al. "How Do Venture Capitalists Make Decisions?" *NBER Working Papers*, Sept. 2016, https://doi.org/10.3386/w22587.

7   Wright, Keith. "Silicon Valley Tech Bubble Is Larger than It Was in 2000, and the End Is Coming." *CNBC*, 22 May 2018, https://www.cnbc.com/2018/05/22/tech-bubble-is-larger-than-in-2000-and-the-end-is-coming.html. Accessed 28 Apr. 2024.

8   Orn, Scott. "Where Do VCs Get Their Money?" *Kruze Consulting*, 16 Mar. 2021, https://kruzeconsulting.com/blog/where-VCs-get-their-money/. Accessed 28 Apr. 2024.

9   Hetler, Amanda. "Tech Sector Layoffs Explained: What You Need to Know." *TechTarget*, 12 Apr. 2023, https://techtarget.com/whatis/feature/Tech-sector-layoffs-explained-What-you-need-to-know. Accessed 28 Apr. 2024.

10  Stringer, Alyssa, and Cody Corrall. "A Comprehensive List of 2023 & 2024 Tech Layoffs." *TechCrunch*, 15 Apr. 2024, https://techcrunch.com/2024/04/15/tech-layoffs-2023-list/. Accessed 28 Apr. 2024.

11  Graham, Paul. "Startup = Growth." *Paulgraham.com*, Sept. 2012, https://paulgraham.com/growth.html. Accessed 28 Apr. 2024.

12  Carey, Scott. "Loot Set out to Disrupt the Banks, Now It's Funded by RBS, What Next?" *Computerworld*, 25 Feb. 2019, https://www.computerworld.com/article/3558320/loot-set-out-to-disrupt-the-banks-now-it-s-funded-by-rbs-what-next.html. Accessed 28 Apr. 2024.

13  O'Hear, Steve. "Loot, the Digital Current Account Aimed at Students and Millennials, Banks £2.2M Series A." *TechCrunch*, 15 Dec. 2017, https://techcrunch.com/2017/12/15/loot/. Accessed 28 Apr. 2024.

14  Greaves, Edmund. "Digital Banking App Loot Goes Bust after It Fails to Secure Financial Backing from RBS." *Interactive Investor*, 22 May 2019, https://www.ii.co.uk/analysis-commentary/digital-banking-app-loot-goes-bust-after-it-fails-secure-financial-backing-rbs-ii512837. Accessed 28 Apr. 2024.

15  Zaleski, Olivia, et al. "Inside Juicero's Demise, from Prized

# NOTES (CHAPTER 1: MIRACLES) 191

Startup to Fire Sale." *Bloomberg.com*, 8 Sept. 2017, https://www.bloomberg.com/news/features/2017-09-08/inside-juicero-s-demise-from-prized-startup-to-fire-sale. Accessed 28 Apr. 2024.

16  Huet, Ellen, and Olivia Zaleski. "Juicero Inc: Silicon Valley Startup Horrified by Discovery of Basic Fault with $400 Juicer." *The Independent*, 20 Apr. 2017, https://www.independent.co.uk/news/business/juicero-inc-silicon-valley-startup-basic-fault-400-juicer-doug-evans-investors-a7692616.html. Accessed 28 Apr. 2024.

17  Bell, Duncan. "Juicero - the Nespresso of Juicing - Is Such a Ridiculous Idea We Assumed It Was an April Fool." *T3*, 21 Apr. 2017, https://www.t3.com/news/juicero-the-nespresso-of-juicing-is-such-a-ridiculous-idea-we-assumed-it-was-an-april-fool. Accessed 28 Apr. 2024.

18  Huet, Ellen, and Olivia Zaleski. "Juicero Inc: Silicon Valley Startup Horrified by Discovery of Basic Fault with $400 Juicer." *The Independent*, 20 Apr. 2017, https://www.independent.co.uk/news/business/juicero-inc-silicon-valley-startup-basic-fault-400-juicer-doug-evans-investors-a7692616.html. Accessed 28 Apr. 2024.

19  Kowitt, Beth. "Startup Selling $400 Juicers Plans to Lower Prices and Cut 25% of Staff." *Fortune*, 14 July 2017, https://fortune.com/2017/07/14/juicero-layoffs-lower-prices/. Accessed 28 Apr. 2024.

20  Reilly, Claire. "Juicero Is Still the Greatest Example of Silicon Valley Stupidity." *CNET*, 1 Sept. 2018, https://www.cnet.com/culture/juicero-is-still-the-greatest-example-of-silicon-valley-stupidity/. Accessed 28 Apr. 2024.

21  "What Happened to Juicero, the $699 Cold Press Juicer?" *Failory*, https://www.failory.com/cemetery/juicero. Accessed 28 Apr. 2024.

22  Zaleski, Olivia, et al. "Inside Juicero's Demise, from Prized Startup to Fire Sale." *Bloomberg.com*, 8 Sept. 2017, https://www.bloomberg.com/news/features/2017-09-08/inside-juicero-s-demise-from-prized-startup-to-fire-sale. Accessed 28 Apr. 2024.

23  "Why Startups Fail: Top 12 Reasons." *CB Insights Research*, 3 Aug. 2021, https://www.cbinsights.com/research/report/startup-failure-reasons-top/. Accessed 28 Apr. 2024.

24 Graham, Paul. "How to Get Startup Ideas." *Paulgraham.com*, Nov. 2012, https://paulgraham.com/startupideas.html. Accessed 28 Apr. 2024.

25 Chowdhury, Hasan. "The VC Dream Machine Pumped out One Dumb Startup after Another. 2023 Should Put an End to That." *Business Insider*, 21 Dec. 2022, https://www.businessinsider.com/2023-should-see-fewer-vc-funded-dumb-ideas-2022-12. Accessed 28 Apr. 2024.

26 Mills, D. Quinn. "Who's to Blame for the Bubble?" *ww*, 1 May 2001, https://hbr.org/2001/05/whos-to-blame-for-the-bubble. Accessed 28 Apr. 2024.

27 BenevolentAI. "BenevolentAI Raises $115 Million to Extend Its Leading Global Position in the Field of AI Enabled Drug Development." *PR Newswire*, 18 Apr. 2018, https://www.prnewswire.com/news-releases/benevolentai-raises-115-million-to-extend-its-leading-global-position-in-the-field-of-ai-enabled-drug-development-680180573.html. Accessed 28 Apr. 2024.

28 *BenevolentAI Annual Report*. 2022, https://www.benevolent.com/application/files/9816/7939/1282/BenevolentAI_Annual_Report_2022.pdf. Accessed 28 Apr. 2024.

29 Lowe, Derek. "BenevolentAI: Worth Two Billion?" *Science*, 23 Apr. 2018, https://www.science.org/content/blog-post/benevolentai-worth-two-billion. Accessed 28 Apr. 2024.

30 Quested, Tony. "BenevolentAI on the Cusp of Greatness." *Business Weekly*, 16 Mar. 2023, https://www.businessweekly.co.uk/posts/benevolentai-on-the-cusp-of-greatness. Accessed 28 Apr. 2024.s

31 Taylor, Nick Paul. "BenevolentAI, Cruel R&D: AI-Enabled Drug Flunks Midphase Eczema Trial to Dent Deal Plans." *FIERCE Biotech*, 5 Apr. 2023, https://www.fiercebiotech.com/biotech/benevolentai-cruel-rd-ai-enabled-drug-flunks-midphase-eczema-trial-dent-deal-plans. Accessed 28 Apr. 2024.

32 Taylor, Nick Paul. "BenevolentAI Makes Deep Cuts after Midphase Flop, Laying off 180 and Shrinking Lab Footprint." *FIERCE Biotech*, 25 May 2023, https://www.fiercebiotech.com/biotech/benevolentai-makes-deep-cuts-after-midphase-flop-laying-180-and-shrinking-lab-footprint. Accessed 28 Apr. 2024.

33 "BenevolentAI Unveils Strategic Plan to Position the Company

for a New Era in AI." *Businesswire*, 25 May 2023, https://www.businesswire.com/news/home/20230524005926/en/BenevolentAI-Unveils-Strategic-Plan-to-Position-the-Company-for-a-New-Era-in-AI. Accessed 28 Apr. 2024.

34 Weitering, Hanneke. "Archer Completes Midnight EVTOL Aircraft Assembly." *Aviation International News*, 11 May 2023, https://www.ainonline.com/news-article/2023-05-11/archer-completes-midnight-evtol-aircraft-assembly. Accessed 28 Apr. 2024.

35 Alcock, Charles. "EVTOL Aircraft Make the Case for Advanced Air Mobility at the Paris Air Show." *Aviation International News*, 19 June 2023, https://www.ainonline.com/news-article/2023-06-20/evtol-aircraft-make-case-advanced-air-mobility-paris-air-show. Accessed 28 Apr. 2024.

36 Blain, Loz. "Second High-Profile Test Flight Crash Rocks EVTOL Industry." *New Atlas*, 15 Aug. 2023, https://newatlas.com/aircraft/vertical-aerospace-evtol-crash/. Accessed 28 Apr. 2024.

37 Weitering, Hanneke. "Archer Aviation Reveals Full-Sized Midnight EVTOL Air Taxi." *Aviation International News*, 17 Nov. 2022, https://www.ainonline.com/news-article/2022-11-16/archer-aviation-reveals-full-sized-midnight-evtol-air-taxi. Accessed 28 Apr. 2024.

38 Weitering, Hanneke. "Archer Completes Midnight EVTOL Aircraft Assembly." *Aviation International News*, 11 May 2023, https://www.ainonline.com/news-article/2023-05-11/archer-completes-midnight-evtol-aircraft-assembly. Accessed 28 Apr. 2024.

39 "First Integrated Vertiport Inaugurated in Paris, Epicentre of Sustainable Advanced Air Mobility (AAM) in Europe." *Groupe ADP*, 10 Nov. 2022, https://presse.groupeadp.fr/first-vertiport-pontoise/?lang=en. Accessed 28 Apr. 2024.

40 Lecca, Tommaso. "Why You Won't Fly in an Air Taxi at the Paris Olympics." *Politico*, 14 Feb. 2024, https://www.politico.eu/article/why-you-wont-fly-air-taxi-paris-olympics/. Accessed 28 Apr. 2024.

41 Johansson, Eric. "Why You Won't Get Flying Cars Any Time Soon." *Verdict*, 8 Nov. 2022, https://www.verdict.co.uk/why-you-wont-get-flying-cars-any-time-soon/. Accessed 28 Apr. 2024.

42  Levin, Tim. "One of Uber's Earliest Investors Says the Billions It Spent on Self-Driving Were a Waste of Money." *Business Insider*, Insider, 2 Feb. 2021, https://www.businessinsider.com/uber-self-driving-waste-of-money-benchmark-bill-gurley-2021-2. Accessed 28 Apr. 2024.

43  Csathy, Peter. "The Case for and against Katzenberg's Quibi." *Forbes*, 12 Aug. 2019, https://www.forbes.com/sites/petercsathy/2019/08/12/the-case-for-and-against-katzenbergs-quibi/. Accessed 28 Apr. 2024.

44  Chmielewski, Dawn. "Coronavirus Lockdown Will Boost Jeff Katzenberg's and Meg Whitman's New Mobile Streaming Service Quibi." *Forbes*, 3 Apr. 2020, https://www.forbes.com/sites/dawnchmielewski/2020/04/03/coronavirus-lockdown-will-boost-jeff-katzenbergs-and-meg-whitmans-new-mobile-streaming-service-quibi/. Accessed 28 Apr. 2024.

45  Berg, Madeline. "Quibi by the Numbers: From Sizzle Reel to Sunken Ship in Less than Seven Months." *Forbes*, 21 Oct. 2020, https://www.forbes.com/sites/maddieberg/2020/10/21/quibi-by-the-numbers-from-sizzle-reel-to-sunken-ship-in-less-than-seven-months/. Accessed 30 Apr. 2024.

46  Byers, Dylan. "Barry Diller Weighs in on the Hollywood Streaming Wars." *NBC News*, 4 Mar. 2020, https://www.nbcnews.com/news/all/barry-diller-weighs-hollywood-streaming-wars-n1149316. Accessed 30 Apr. 2024.

47  Wallace, Benjamin. "Is Anyone Watching Quibi?" *Vulture*, 6 July 2020, https://www.vulture.com/2020/07/is-anyone-watching-quibi.html. Accessed 30 Apr. 2024.

48  Lee, Benjamin. "Quibi Review – Shortform Sub-Netflix Shows Aren't Long for This World." *The Guardian*, 6 Apr. 2020, https://www.theguardian.com/tv-and-radio/2020/apr/06/quibi-streaming-review-short-form-tv. Accessed 30 Apr. 2024.

49  VanArendonk, Kathryn. "Yep, Quibi Is Bad." *Vulture*, 24 Apr. 2020, https://www.vulture.com/2020/04/the-bites-are-quick-and-bad.html. Accessed 30 Apr. 2024.

50  Wallace, Benjamin. "Is Anyone Watching Quibi?" *Vulture*, 6 July 2020, https://www.vulture.com/2020/07/is-anyone-watching-quibi.html. Accessed 30 Apr. 2024.

51  Koetsier, John. "Massive TikTok Growth: Up 75% This Year,

## NOTES (CHAPTER 1: MIRACLES) 195

Now 33X More Users than Nearest Direct Competitor." *Forbes*, 14 Sept. 2020, https://www.forbes.com/sites/johnkoetsier/2020/09/14/massive-tiktok-growth-up-75-this-year-now-33x-more-users-than-nearest-competitor/. Accessed 30 Apr. 2024.

52  Boorstin, Julia, and Steve Kovach. "Quibi Officially Announces It's Shutting Down." *CNBC*, 21 Oct. 2020, https://www.cnbc.com/2020/10/21/quibi-to-shut-down-after-just-6-months.html.

53  Berg, Madeline. "Quibi by the Numbers: From Sizzle Reel to Sunken Ship in Less than Seven Months." *Forbes*, 21 Oct. 2020, https://www.forbes.com/sites/maddieberg/2020/10/21/quibi-by-the-numbers-from-sizzle-reel-to-sunken-ship-in-less-than-seven-months/. Accessed 30 Apr. 2024.

54  "An Open Letter from Quibi," 21 Oct. 2020, https://quibi-hq.medium.com/an-open-letter-from-quibi-8af6b415377f. Accessed 30 Apr. 2024.

55  García-Hodges, Ahiza. "Quibi Is Shutting down Just Months after Launching." *NBC News*, 22 Oct. 2020, https://www.nbcnews.com/news/all/quibi-shutting-down-just-months-after-launching-n1244215. Accessed 30 Apr. 2024.

56  *Future Fund Management Agency, Australian Government.* https://www.futurefund.gov.au/. Accessed 30 Apr. 2024.

57  Patrick, Aaron. "Future Fund Invested in Failed Quibi Streaming Service." *Australian Financial Review*, 22 Oct. 2020, https://www.afr.com/technology/future-fund-invested-in-failed-quibi-streaming-service-20201023-p567u6. Accessed 30 Apr. 2024.

58  Hermann, Jaryd. "Why Quibi Died: The $2B Dumpster Fire That Was Supposed to Revolutionize Hollywood." *How They Grow*, 14 June 2023, https://www.howtheygrow.co/p/why-quibi-died-the-2b-dumpster-fire. Accessed 30 Apr. 2024.

59  Smith, Tim, and Amy Lewin. "See the Pitch Memo That Raised €105m for Four-Week-Old Startup Mistral." *Sifted*, 21 June 2023, https://sifted.eu/articles/pitch-deck-mistral. Accessed 30 Apr. 2024.

60  Ibid.

61  Ibid.

62  Lunden, Ingrid. "France's Mistral AI Blows in with a $113M Seed Round at a $260M Valuation to Take on OpenAI."

*TechCrunch*, 13 June 2023, https://techcrunch.com/2023/06/13/frances-mistral-ai-blows-in-with-a-113m-seed-round-at-a-260m-valuation-to-take-on-openai/. Accessed 30 Apr. 2024.

63 "Month-Old AI Startup Mistral Raises $113 Million." *PYMNTS*, 14 June 2023, https://www.pymnts.com/news/investment-tracker/2023/month-old-ai-startup-mistral-raises-113-million/. Accessed 30 Apr. 2024.

64 Guest, Peter. "Why Silicon Valley Falls for Frauds." *Wired*, 2 Oct. 2023, https://www.wired.com/story/why-silicon-valley-falls-for-frauds/. Accessed 30 Apr. 2024.

65 Guest, Peter. "Why Silicon Valley Falls for Frauds." *Wired*, 2 Oct. 2023, https://www.wired.com/story/why-silicon-valley-falls-for-frauds/. Accessed 30 Apr. 2024.

66 Masters, Brooke. "Doesn't Anyone Do Due Diligence Any More?" *Financial Times*, 30 Nov. 2022, https://www.ft.com/content/e739d9ed-b8ee-4d8e-ad29-0d01889d5775. Accessed 30 Apr. 2024.

67 Williams-Grut, Oscar. "Loot Raises £1.5 Million to Build a Bank for 'Generation Snapchat.'" *Business Insider*, 21 June 2016, https://www.businessinsider.com/loot-raises-series-a-rocket-internet-bank-for-millennials-2016-6. Accessed 30 Apr. 2024.

68 Ford Rojas, Jean-Paul. "Rishi Sunak to Offload Further Chunk of State-Backed NatWest over next 12 Months." *Sky News*, 22 July 2022, https://news.sky.com/story/treasury-to-offload-up-to-15-of-state-backed-natwest-over-next-12-months-12361034. Accessed 30 Apr. 2024.

69 Bradbury, Rosie. "Calpers Ups vc Allocation after Lost Decade." *PitchBook*, 11 Jan. 2023, https://pitchbook.com/news/articles/calpers-venture-asset-class-tiger-lightspeed. Accessed 30 Apr. 2024.

70 Haque, Jennah, and Marvis Gutierrez. "Crypto Fallout Leaves US Retiree Benefits Mostly Unscathed." *Bloomberg.com*, 18 Nov. 2022, https://www.bloomberg.com/news/articles/2022-11-18/crypto-fallout-leaves-us-retiree-benefits-mostly-unscathed. Accessed 30 Apr. 2024.

71 Cumbo, Josephine. "Calpers Plans Multibillion-Dollar Push into Venture Capital." *Financial Times*, 12 June 2023, https://www.ft.com/content/86b49e10-3dd2-4427-b70b-993bad47b061. Accessed 30 Apr. 2024.

72  Jacobius, Arleen. "Afore XXI Banorte Targets $1 Billion in International Private Equity, Real Estate." *Pensions & Investments*, 2 May 2018, https://www.pionline.com/article/20180502/ONLINE/180509972/afore-xxi-banorte-targets-1-billion-in-international-private-equity-real-estate. Accessed 30 Apr. 2024.

## CHAPTER 2: EXPLOSIVE GROWTH

1  Duhigg, Charles. "How Venture Capitalists Are Deforming Capitalism." *The New Yorker*, 23 Nov. 2020, https://www.newyorker.com/magazine/2020/11/30/how-venture-capitalists-are-deforming-capitalism. Accessed 30 Apr. 2024.

2  Wansley, Matthew, and Samuel Weinstein. "Venture Predation." *Cardozo Legal Studies Research Paper, No. 708*, Jan. 2023, https://doi.org/10.2139/ssrn.4437360. Accessed 30 Apr. 2024.

3  Molla, Rani. "Why Companies like Lyft and Uber Are Going Public without Having Profits." *Vox*, 6 Mar. 2019, https://www.vox.com/2019/3/6/18249997/lyft-uber-ipo-public-profit. Accessed 30 Apr. 2024.

4  Ritter, Jay R. "Initial Public Offerings: Updated Statistics." *Warrington College of Business*, 26 Apr. 2024, https://site.warrington.ufl.edu/ritter/files/IPO-Statistics.pdf. Accessed 30 Apr. 2024.

5  Billing, Mimi, et al. "Struggling Scooter Scaleup Tier Raises Convertible Note from Existing Investors as It Looks for a Buyer." *Sifted*, 16 May 2023, https://sifted.eu/articles/escooter-tier-convertible-note-investors-buyer-news. Accessed 30 Apr. 2024.

6  Mendel, Jack. "Dott Ends London E-Bike Service due to 'High Fees and Varied Regulations.'" *CityAM*, 22 Sept. 2023, https://www.cityam.com/dott-ends-london-e-bike-service-due-to-high-fees-and-varied-regulations/. Accessed 30 Apr. 2024.

7  Duhigg, Charles. "How Venture Capitalists Are Deforming Capitalism." *The New Yorker*, 23 Nov. 2020, https://www.newyorker.com/magazine/2020/11/30/how-venture-capitalists-are-deforming-capitalism. Accessed 30 Apr. 2024.

8   See discussion here: https://twitter.com/lennysan/status/1314237584952881152. Accessed 30 Apr.

9   Raval, Anjli. "WeWork Looking to Share Its Plans for Coworking beyond US Borders." *Financial Times*, 11 Mar. 2024, https://www.ft.com/content/5bd2bc20-a862-11e3-8ce1-00144feab7de. Accessed 30 Apr. 2024.

10  Nicolaou, Anna. "WeWork Cultivating 'Physical Social Network.'" *Financial Times*, 17 Mar. 2016, https://www.ft.com/content/f2e073a2-d0ef-11e5-831d-09f7778e7377. Accessed 30 Apr. 2024.

11  "WeWork Amenities." *WeWork*, https://www.wework.com/en-GB/l/coworking-space/central-london--london#amenities-full/. Accessed 30 Apr. 2024.

12  Ockwell, Bif. "The Community Teams at the Heart of Every WeWork." *Ideas*, 8 Dec. 2022, https://www.wework.com/ideas/community-stories/employee-spotlight/the-community-teams-at-the-heart-of-every-wework. Accessed 30 Apr. 2024.

13  Rice, Andrew. "Is This the Office of the Future or a $5 Billion Waste of Space?" *Bloomberg*, 21 May 2015, https://www.bloomberg.com/news/features/2015-05-21/wework-real-estate-empire-or-shared-office-space-for-a-new-era-. Accessed 30 Apr. 2024.

14  Brown, Eliot. "WeWork: A $20 Billion Startup Fueled by Silicon Valley Pixie Dust." *Wall Street Journal*, 19 Oct. 2017, https://www.wsj.com/articles/wework-a-20-billion-startup-fueled-by-silicon-valley-pixie-dust-1508424483. Accessed 30 Apr. 2024.

15  Nicolaou, Anna. "WeWork Cultivating 'Physical Social Network.'" *Financial Times*, 17 Mar. 2016, https://www.ft.com/content/f2e073a2-d0ef-11e5-831d-09f7778e7377. Accessed 30 Apr.

16  "WeWork S-1 Form." *SEC*, 14 Aug. 2019, https://www.sec.gov/Archives/edgar/data/1533523/000119312519220499/d781982ds1.htm. Accessed 30 Apr. 2024.

17  Brown, Eliot, and Maureen Farell. "Former WeWork Chief's Gargantuan Exit Package Gets New Sweetener." *Wall Street Journal*, 27 May 2021, https://www.wsj.com/articles/former-wework-chiefs-gargantuan-exit-package-gets-new-sweetener-11622115000. Accessed 30 Apr. 2024.

## NOTES (CHAPTER 2: GROWTH)

18  *WeWork Investor Presentation.* 11 Oct. 2019, https://www.wework.com/ideas/wp-content/uploads/2019/11/Investor-Presentation%E2%80%94October-2019.pdf. Slide 6. Accessed 30 Apr. 2024.

19  Huet, Ellen. "WeWork Offices Are Now Just as Full as They Were before the Pandemic." *Bloomberg*, 4 Aug. 2022, https://www.bloomberg.com/news/articles/2022-08-04/wework-we-earnings-occupancy-rate-matches-pre-pandemic-level. Accessed 30 Apr. 2024.

20  Perez, Sarah. "Hopper's New Travel App Tells You the Best Time to Fly." *TechCrunch*, 28 Jan. 2015, https://techcrunch.com/2015/01/28/hoppers-new-travel-app-tells-you-the-best-time-to-fly/. Accessed 30 Apr. 2024.

21  Hinchliffe, Emma. "Hopper Raises $62 Million in Its Bid to Take over Travel." *Mashable*, 15 Dec. 2016, https://mashable.com/article/hopper-travel-app-series-c. Accessed 30 Apr. 2024.

22  Hoefling, Brian. "Hopper Aiming for More Transparent Travel Search." *Boston Business Journal*, 5 Oct. 2024, https://www.bizjournals.com/boston/blog/startups/2014/10/hopper-aiming-for-more-transparent-travel-search.html. Accessed 30 Apr. 2024.

23  Schaal, Dennis. "Exclusive: Expedia Terminates Its Hopper Relationship, Says It 'Exploits Consumer Anxiety.'" *Skift*, 12 July 2023, https://skift.com/2023/07/12/exclusive-expedia-terminates-its-hopper-relationship-says-it-exploits-consumer-anxiety/. Accessed 30 Apr. 2024.

24  Schaal, Dennis. "Exclusive: Hopper Terminates Booking.com Partnership in Preemptive Strike." *Skift*, 6 Oct. 2023, https://skift.com/2023/10/06/exclusive-hopper-terminates-booking-com-partnership-in-preemptive-strike/. Accessed 30 Apr. 2024.

25  Greenwald, Bruce C. *Value Investing: From Graham to Buffett and Beyond.* Wiley, 2004, p. 76.

26  Hu, Krystal. "ChatGPT Sets Record for Fastest-Growing User Base." *Reuters*, 2 Feb. 2023, https://www.reuters.com/technology/chatgpt-sets-record-fastest-growing-user-base-analyst-note-2023-02-01/. Accessed 30 Apr. 2024.

27  Vaswani, Ashish, et al. "Attention Is All You Need," 12 June 2017, https://arxiv.org/abs/1706.03762.

28  Patel, Dylan, and Afzal Ahmad. "Google 'We Have No Moat,

and Neither Does OpenAI.'" *SemiAnalysis*, 4 May 2023, https://www.semianalysis.com/p/google-we-have-no-moat-and-neither. Accessed 30 Apr. 2024.

29  Thiel, Peter, and Blake Masters. *Zero to One: Notes on Startups, or How to Build the Future*. Virgin Books, 2014, p. 48.

30  Corbishley, Chris. *Does Your Startup Pass the 10x Test?* 24 Apr. 2019, https://www.linkedin.com/pulse/does-your-startup-pass-10x-test-chris-corbishley-macbain/. Accessed 30 Apr. 2024.

31  Vincent, James. "Meta's Powerful AI Language Model Has Leaked Online — What Happens Now?" *The Verge*, 8 Mar. 2023, https://www.theverge.com/2023/3/8/23629362/meta-ai-language-model-llama-leak-online-misuse. Accessed 30 Apr. 2024.

32  Shazeer, Noam M., et al. "Attention-Based Sequence Transduction Neural Networks." *US Patent*, 28 June 2018, https://patents.google.com/patent/US10452978B2/en.

33  See, for example, Hamilton Helmer. *7 Powers: The Foundations of Business Strategy*. Deep Strategy, 2016.

34  Thiel, Peter, and Blake Masters. *Zero to One: Notes on Startups, or How to Build the Future*. Virgin Books, 2014, p. 51.

35  Greenwald, Bruce C., and Judd Kahn. *Competition Demystified*. Penguin, 2005, p. 38.

36  Greenwald, Bruce C., and Judd Kahn. *Competition Demystified*. Penguin, 2005, p. 39.

37  Fowler, Geoffrey A. "Google Spent $26 Billion to Hide This Phone Setting from You." *Washington Post*, 8 Nov. 2023, https://www.washingtonpost.com/technology/2023/11/08/google-search-default-iphone-samsung/. Accessed 30 Apr. 2024.

38  Pierce, David. "Google Paid a Whopping $26.3 Billion in 2021 to Be the Default Search Engine Everywhere." *The Verge*, 27 Oct. 2023, https://www.theverge.com/2023/10/27/23934961/google-antitrust-trial-defaults-search-deal-26-3-billion. Accessed 30 Apr. 2024.

39  Dodds, Io. "Is WeWork the Office of the Future – or an Overvalued Confidence Trick?" *The Telegraph*, 15 Aug. 2019, https://www.telegraph.co.uk/technology/2019/08/15/47bn-wework-office-future-overvalued-confidence-trick/. Accessed 30 Apr. 2024.

40  Greenwald, Bruce C. *Value Investing: From Graham to Buffett and Beyond*. Wiley, 2004. "Chapter 5: Earnings Power Value."

41  Hamilton Helmer. *7 Powers: The Foundations of Business Strategy*. Deep Strategy, 2016.

42  Greenwald, Bruce C. *Value Investing: From Graham to Buffett and Beyond*. Wiley, 2004. "Chapter 6: A wonderful little franchise."

## CHAPTER 3: VENTURE CAPITAL

1  Flickinger, Mark. "Venture Capital Fundamentals: Why vc Is a Driving Force of Innovation." *Forbes*, 29 Mar. 2023, https://www.forbes.com/sites/markflickinger/2023/03/29/venture-capital-fundamentals-why-vc-is-a-driving-force-of-innovation/. Accessed 30 Apr. 2024.

2  "Charlie Munger (Podcast Transcript)." *Acquired*, 29 Oct. 2023, https://www.acquired.fm/episodes/charlie-munger. Accessed 30 Apr. 2024.

3  Gornall, Will, and Ilya A. Strebulaev. "Squaring Venture Capital Valuations with Reality." *NBER Working Papers*, Oct. 2017, https://www.nber.org/system/files/working_papers/w23895/w23895.pdf.

4  Laine, Markus and Torstila, Sami (2005) "The Exit Rates of Liquidated Venture Capital Funds," *Journal of Entrepreneurial Finance and Business Ventures*. DOI: https://doi.org/10.57229/2373-1761.1225.

5  Silber, Jordan. "What You Need to Know about Erisa and Accepting Capital Commitments from 'Benefit Plan' Investors." *TheFundLawyer*, 9 Mar. 2018, https://thefundlawyer.cooley.com/erisa-capital-commitments-benefit-plan-investors/. Accessed 30 Apr. 2024.

6  Wilson, Fred. "What Is a Good Venture Return?" *AVC*, 20 Mar. 2009, https://avc.com/2009/03/what-is-a-good-venture-return/. Accessed 30 Apr. 2024.

7  See, e.g., https://www.officialdata.org/us/stocks/s-p-500/1957?amount=100&endYear=2023. At 10.26% a year, we obtain a total compounded return of 1.6x in a five-year period ($1.1^5 \approx 1.6$).

8   Wilson, Fred. "What Is a Good Venture Return?" *AVC*, 20 Mar. 2009, https://avc.com/2009/03/what-is-a-good-venture-return/. Accessed 30 Apr. 2024.

9   Gutman, Collin. "Explaining vc Math: Is Your Idea Big Enough?" 24 July 2019, https://medium.com/@collinhgutman/explaining-vc-math-is-your-idea-big-enough-5079390ae788. Accessed 30 Apr. 2024.

10  Taulli, Tom. "Pitching a VC: How to Size the Market Opportunity." *Forbes*, 1 June 2019, https://www.forbes.com/sites/tomtaulli/2019/01/06/pitching-a-vc-how-to-size-the-market-opportunity/. Accessed 30 Apr. 2024.

11  Thiel, Peter, and Blake Masters. *Zero to One: Notes on Startups, or How to Build the Future*. Virgin Books, 2014. Chapter 7.

12  Evans, Benedict. *In Praise of Failure*. 10 Aug. 2016, https://www.ben-evans.com/benedictevans/2016/4/28/winning-and-losing. Accessed 30 Apr. 2024.

13  Grimes, Ann. "Venture Capitalists Scramble To Keep Their Numbers Secret." *Wall Street Journal*, 11 May 2004, https://www.wsj.com/articles/SB108422642755407319. Accessed 30 Apr. 2024.

14  Cambridge Associates. *US Venture Capital, Index and Selected Benchmark Statistics*. 30 June 2020, https://www.cambridgeassociates.com/wp-content/uploads/2020/11/WEB-2020-Q2-USVC-Benchmark-Book.pdf. Accessed 30 Apr. 2024.

15  Harris, Robert S., et al. "Has Persistence Persisted in Private Equity? Evidence from Buyout and Venture Capital Funds." *Journal of Corporate Finance*, Feb. 2023, https://doi.org/10.1016/j.jcorpfin.2023.102361.

16  Prencipe, Dario. *The European Venture Capital Landscape: An EIF Perspective, Volume III: Liquidity Events and Returns of EIF-Backed VC Investments*. Apr. 2017, https://www.fi-compass.eu/sites/default/files/publications/eif_wp_41.pdf. Accessed 30 Apr. 2024.

17  Coats, David. *Venture Capital — No, We're Not Normal*. 11 Sept. 2019, https://medium.com/correlation-ventures/venture-capital-no-were-not-normal-32a26edea7c7. Accessed 1 May 2024.

18  We know returns were in the range 0x–1x. It's been argued that

# NOTES (CHAPTER 3: VENTURE CAPITAL) 203

in most cases they were probably closer to 0x than 1x (see https://www.sethlevine.com/archives/2014/08/venture-outcomes-are-even-more-skewed-than-you-think.html).

19  Hinduja, Karam. "The Venture-Capital Bubble Is Going to Burst." *Barrons*, 20 Mar. 2019, https://www.barrons.com/articles/the-vc-bubble-is-going-to-burst-51553077853. Accessed 30 Apr. 2024.

20  FMVA, Fredrick D. Scott. "Why Power Law Portfolio Construction Will Always Be Dead on Arrival in the Venture Capital Industry." *Entrepreneur*, 3 June 2022, https://www.entrepreneur.com/money-finance/why-power-law-portfolio-construction-will-always-be-dead-on/426811. Accessed 30 Apr. 2024.

21  Farha, Dany. "Understanding the vc Business Model." *Entrepreneur*, 29 May 2016, https://www.entrepreneur.com/en-ae/finance/understanding-the-vc-business-model/276639. Accessed 30 Apr. 2024.

22  Harris, Robert S., et al. "Has Persistence Persisted in Private Equity? Evidence from Buyout and Venture Capital Funds." *Journal of Corporate Finance*, Feb. 2023, https://doi.org/10.1016/j.jcorpfin.2023.102361.

23  Harris, Robert S., et al. "Has Persistence Persisted in Private Equity? Evidence from Buyout and Venture Capital Funds." *Journal of Corporate Finance*, Feb. 2023, https://doi.org/10.1016/j.jcorpfin.2023.102361.

24  Nanda, Ramana, et al. "The Persistent Effect of Initial Success: Evidence from Venture Capital." *Journal of Financial Economics*, vol. 137, no. 1, Feb. 2020, https://doi.org/10.1016/j.jfineco.2020.01.004.

25  Mulcahy, Diane, et al. *We Have Met the Enemy...and He Is Us: Lessons from Twenty Years of the Kauffman Foundation's Investments in Venture Capital Funds and the Triumph of Hope over Experience.* May 2012, p. 28, https://doi.org/10.2139/ssrn.2053258.

26  Newcomer, Eric, and Jessica Matthews. "Inside Andreessen Horowitz's Grand Plans to Scale Its Venture Capital Firm into a Behemoth and Conquer the Globe." *Fortune*, 23 Nov. 2022, https://fortune.com/longform/andreessen-horowitz-beyond-silicon-valley/. Accessed 30 Apr. 2024.

27 See:
a) Sender, Henny. "Sequoia Capital Closes First Round on $8bn Global Fund." *Financial Times*, 26 June 2018, https://www.ft.com/content/2fd281f2-775a-11e8-8e67-1e1a0846c475. Accessed 30 Apr. 2024.
b) Clark, Kate, and Jonathan Shieber. "Setting Politics Aside, Sequoia Raises $3.4 Billion for US and China Investments." *TechCrunch*, 4 Dec. 2019, https://techcrunch.com/2019/12/03/setting-politics-aside-sequoia-raises-3-4-billion-for-us-and-china-investments/. Accessed 30 Apr. 2024.
c) *TechCrunch*, 4 Dec. 2019, https://techcrunch.com/2019/12/03/setting-politics-aside-sequoia-raises-3-4-billion-for-us-and-china-investments/. Accessed 30 Apr. 2024.
d) Louch, Yuliya Chernova and William. "Sequoia Capital Is in No Rush to Spend $8 Billion Fund." *Wall Street Journal*, 10 Jan. 2020, https://www.wsj.com/articles/sequoia-is-in-no-rush-to-spend-8-billion-fund-11578654000. Accessed 30 Apr. 2024.
e) Chen, Lulu Yilun. "Sequoia China Raises $9 Billion as Investors Flock to Big Funds." *Bloomberg*, 5 July 2022, https://www.bloomberg.com/news/articles/2022-07-05/sequoia-china-raises-9-billion-as-investors-flock-to-big-funds. Accessed 30 Apr. 2024.

28 Feld, Brad, and Jason Mendelson. *Venture Deals: Be Smarter than Your Lawyer and Venture Capitalist*. 3rd ed., Wiley, 2016, p. 134.

29 Zweig, Jason. "A Fireside Chat with Charlie Munger." *Wall Street Journal*, 12 Sept. 2014, https://www.wsj.com/articles/BL-MBB-26843. Accessed 30 Apr. 2024.

30 Mulcahy, Diane, et al. *We Have Met the Enemy…and He Is Us: Lessons from Twenty Years of the Kauffman Foundation's Investments in Venture Capital Funds and the Triumph of Hope over Experience*. May 2012, p. 4, https://doi.org/10.2139/ssrn.2053258.

31 Newcomer, Eric, and Jessica Matthews. "Inside Andreessen Horowitz's Grand Plans to Scale Its Venture Capital Firm into a Behemoth and Conquer the Globe." *Fortune*, 23 Nov. 2022, https://fortune.com/longform/andreessen-horowitz-beyond-silicon-valley/. Accessed 30 Apr. 2024.

32 Litvak, Kate (2009) "Venture Capital Limited Partnership Agreements: Understanding Compensation Arrangements," *University of Chicago Law Review*: Vol. 76: Iss.

# NOTES (CHAPTER 3: VENTURE CAPITAL) 205

1, Article 7. Available at: https://chicagounbound.uchicago.edu/uclrev/vol76/iss1/7.

33  Palihapitiya, Chamath. "2018 Annual Letter." *Social Capital*, 2018, https://www.socialcapital.com/ideas/2018-annual-letter. Accessed 30 Apr. 2024.

34  Mulcahy, Diane, et al. *We Have Met the Enemy…and He Is Us: Lessons from Twenty Years of the Kauffman Foundation's Investments in Venture Capital Funds and the Triumph of Hope over Experience.* May 2012, p. 34, https://doi.org/10.2139/ssrn.2053258.

35  Brown, Gregory W., et al. "Do Private Equity Funds Manipulate Reported Returns?" *Journal of Financial Economics*, vol. 132, no. 2, May 2019, pp. 267–97, https://doi.org/10.1016/j.jfineco.2018.10.011.

36  Kupor, Scott. "When Is a 'Mark' Not a Mark? When It's a Venture Capital Mark." *Andreessen Horowitz*, 1 Sept. 2016, https://a16z.com/when-is-a-mark-not-a-mark-when-its-a-venture-capital-mark/. Accessed 30 Apr. 2024.

37  Bradbury, Rosie. "Down Rounds Are Rising. History Shows Things Could Get Much Worse." *PitchBook*, 25 Sept. 2023, https://pitchbook.com/news/articles/down-rounds-venture-fundraising-vc-deals-recession. Accessed 30 Apr. 2024.

38  Palihapitiya, Chamath. "2018 Annual Letter." *Social Capital*, 2018, https://www.socialcapital.com/ideas/2018-annual-letter. Accessed 30 Apr. 2024.

39  Suppose a fund exits two start-up investments for a 2.5x return after five years. If you do the math, this generates an IRR of 20%. If the fund exits one of the two start-ups earlier, after only three years, the IRR is 33%.

40  Mulcahy, Diane, et al. *We Have Met the Enemy…and He Is Us: Lessons from Twenty Years of the Kauffman Foundation's Investments in Venture Capital Funds and the Triumph of Hope over Experience.* May 2012, p. 4, https://doi.org/10.2139/ssrn.2053258.

41  Phalippou, Ludovic. "An Inconvenient Fact: Private Equity Returns & the Billionaire Factory." *University of Oxford, Said Business School, Working Paper*, 2020, https://doi.org/10.2139/ssrn.3623820.

42  Bogan, Vicki. *The Greater Fool Theory: What Is It?* http://bogan.

dyson.cornell.edu/doc/Hartford/Bogan-9_GreaterFools.pdf. Accessed 30 Apr. 2024.

43 Hinduja, Karam. "The Venture-Capital Bubble Is Going to Burst." *Barrons*, 20 Mar. 2019, https://www.barrons.com/articles/the-vc-bubble-is-going-to-burst-51553077853. Accessed 30 Apr.

44 Kar, Ayushi. "Start-up Funding Becoming like a Ponzi Scheme: Narayana Murthy." *BusinessLine*, 2 Mar. 2023, https://www.thehindubusinessline.com/companies/start-up-funding-becoming-like-a-ponzi-scheme-narayana-murthy/article66572578.ece. Accessed 30 Apr. 2024.

45 Sheik, Sherwin. "The Displacement of Tom Perkins with the Greater Fool Theory." *HuffPost*, 17 June 2016, https://www.huffpost.com/entry/the-displacement-of-tom-p_b_10517774. Accessed 30 Apr. 2024.

46 Fisher, Adam. "Sam Bankman-Fried Has a Savior Complex—and Maybe You Should Too." *Sequoia*, 22 Sept. 2022, https://web.archive.org/web/20221027181005/https://www.sequoiacap.com/article/sam-bankman-fried-spotlight/.

47 Allyn, Bobby. "The Elizabeth Holmes Trial Is Sparking a Gender Debate in Silicon Valley." *NPR*, 24 Sept. 2021, https://www.npr.org/2021/09/24/1040353540/the-elizabeth-holmes-trial-is-sparking-a-gender-debate. Accessed 1 May 2024.

48 Gurley, Bill. "In Defense of the Deck." *Above the Crowd*, 7 July 2015, https://abovethecrowd.com/2015/07/07/in-defense-of-the-deck/. Accessed 1 May 2024.

49 Nitasha Tiku. "WeWork Used These Documents to Convince Investors It's Worth Billions." *BuzzFeed News*, 9 Oct. 2015, https://www.buzzfeednews.com/article/nitashatiku/how-wework-convinced-investors-its-worth-billions. Accessed 1 May 2024.

50 Sorkin, Andrew Ross. "Adam Neumann's New Company Gets a Big Check from Andreessen Horowitz." *The New York Times*, 15 Aug. 2022, https://www.nytimes.com/2022/08/15/business/dealbook/adam-neumann-wework-startup.html. Accessed 1 May 2024.

51 Andreessen, Marc. "Investing in Flow." *Andreessen Horowitz*, 15 Aug. 2022, https://a16z.com/announcement/investing-in-flow/. Accessed 1 May 2024.

52  Hinduja, Karam. "The Venture-Capital Bubble Is Going to Burst." *Barrons*, 20 Mar. 2019, https://www.barrons.com/articles/the-vc-bubble-is-going-to-burst-51553077853. Accessed 30 Apr. 2024.

53  Lopez, Linette. "AI Is Silicon Valley's Desperate, Last-Ditch Attempt to Avoid a Stock Market Wipeout." *Business Insider*, 7 May 2023, https://www.businessinsider.com/ai-technology-chatgpt-silicon-valley-save-business-stock-market-jobs-2023-5. Accessed 1 May 2024.

54  Masters, Brooke. "Doesn't Anyone Do Due Diligence Any More?" *Financial Times*, 30 Nov. 2022, https://www.ft.com/content/e739d9ed-b8ee-4d8e-ad29-0d01889d5775. Accessed 30 Apr.

55  Mulcahy, Diane, et al. *We Have Met the Enemy…and He Is Us: Lessons from Twenty Years of the Kauffman Foundation's Investments in Venture Capital Funds and the Triumph of Hope over Experience.* May 2012, p. 16, https://doi.org/10.2139/ssrn.2053258.

56  Palihapitiya, Chamath. "2018 Annual Letter." *Social Capital*, 2018, https://www.socialcapital.com/ideas/2018-annual-letter. Accessed 30 Apr. 2024.

## CHAPTER 4: CHEAP MONEY, FREE MONEY

1  Wigglesworth, Robin. "ZIRP: Good, Actually!" *Financial Times*, 19 Sept. 2023, https://www.ft.com/content/77b98af7-4089-4d1e-9eb1-e42053813aa2. Accessed 1 May 2024.

2  Joyce, Michael et al. "The United Kingdom's Quantitative Easing Policy: Design, Operation and Impact." *Bank of England Quarterly Bulletin,* 19 Sept. 2011, Available at SSRN: https://ssrn.com/abstract=1933696.

3  Gagnon, Joseph, et al. *The Financial Market Effects of the Federal Reserve's Large-Scale Asset Purchases.* International Journal of Central Banking, 2011, https://www.ijcb.org/journal/ijcb11q1a1.pdf.

4  Adrian, Tobias (speech by). First Annual Bank of England Agenda for Research (BEAR) Conference: The Monetary Toolkit. 24 Feb. 2022, https://www.imf.org/-/media/Files/News/

Speech/2022/sp-022422-first-annual-bank-of-england-agenda-for-research-conference.ashx. Accessed 30 Apr. 2024.

5   Adrian, Tobias. "'Low for Long' and Risk-Taking." *IMF*, 24 Nov. 2020, https://www.imf.org/en/Publications/Departmental-Papers-Policy-Papers/Issues/2020/11/23/Low-for-Long-and-Risk-Taking-49733. Accessed 1 May 2024.

6   "Quantitative Easing: A Dangerous Addiction?" *House of Lords, Economic Affairs Committee*, 16 July 2021, https://committees.parliament.uk/publications/6725/documents/71894/default/. Accessed 1 May 2024.

7   The balance in HSBC's account at the Fed would be increased by the same amount as the pension fund's balance at HSBC. There would be intermediaries in the process though, such as bond dealers. See: Wang, Joseph. "Quantitative Easing Step-By-Step." *FedGuy.com*, 19 Sept. 2020, https://fedguy.com/quantitative-easing-step-by-step/. Accessed 1 May 2024.

8   Board of Governors of the Federal Reserve System (US), Demand Deposits [DEMDEPNS]. https://fred.stlouisfed.org/graph/?g=1o1kE

9   Castro, Andrew, et al. "Understanding Bank Deposit Growth during the COVID-19 Pandemic." *Federal Reserve*, June 2022, https://www.federalreserve.gov/econres/notes/feds-notes/understanding-bank-deposit-growth-during-the-covid-19-pandemic-20220603.html. Accessed 1 May 2024.

10  Leonard, Christopher. *The Lords of Easy Money: How the Federal Reserve Broke the American Economy*. Simon & Schuster, 2022. Chapter 3.

11  Doherty, Brian et al. "Whatever Happened to Inflation?" *Reason*, 30 Nov. 2014, https://reason.com/2014/11/30/whatever-happened-to-inflation/. Accessed 1 May 2024.

12  Lopez, German. "Inflation and Price Gouging." *The New York Times*, 14 June 2022, https://www.nytimes.com/2022/06/14/briefing/inflation-supply-chain-greedflation.html. Accessed 1 May 2024.

13  Conway, Ed. "Cost of Living: Bank of England Shares Responsibility for Crisis, Former Governor Says." *Sky News*, 20 May 2022, https://news.sky.com/story/cost-of-living-bank-of-england-shares-responsibility-for-crisis-former-governor-says-12617190. Accessed 1 May 2024.

NOTES (CHAPTER 4: CHEAP MONEY)   209

14  Goodwin, Tom. "The Battle Is for the Customer Interface." *TechCrunch*, 3 Mar. 2015, https://techcrunch.com/2015/03/03/in-the-age-of-disintermediation-the-battle-is-all-for-the-customer-interface/. Accessed 1 May 2024..

15  Hern, Alex. "TechScape: The End of the 'Free Money' Era." *The Guardian*, 11 Apr. 2023, https://www.theguardian.com/technology/2023/apr/11/techscape-zirp-tech-boom. Accessed 1 May 2024.

16  Masters, Brooke. "Doesn't Anyone Do Due Diligence Any More?" *Financial Times*, 30 Nov. 2022, https://www.ft.com/content/e739d9ed-b8ee-4d8e-ad29-0d01889d5775. Accessed 30 Apr. 2024.

17  Mims, Christopher. "After a Sugar High of Free Money, These Billion-Dollar Technologies Need a Nap." *Wall Street Journal*, 11 Jan. 2024, https://www.wsj.com/tech/personal-tech/after-a-sugar-high-of-free-money-these-billion-dollar-technologies-need-a-nap-dc4c4b20. Accessed 1 May 2024.

18  Goswami, Rohan. "Startup Bubble Fueled by Fed's Cheap Money Policy Finally Burst in 2023." *CNBC*, 28 Dec. 2023, https://www.cnbc.com/2023/12/28/startup-bubble-fueled-by-fed-cheap-money-policy-finally-burst-in-2023.html. Accessed 1 May 2024.

19  Maloney, Tom et al. "SVB's Loans Underpinned Venture Capital Boom That's Now Busting." *Bloomberg*, 22 Mar. 2023, https://www.bloomberg.com/news/articles/2023-03-22/svb-s-loans-underpinned-venture-capital-boom-that-s-now-busting. Accessed 1 May 2024.

20  Hu, Krystal. "Venture Capital Funding Plunges Globally in First Half despite AI Frenzy." *Reuters*, 6 July 2023, https://www.reuters.com/business/finance/venture-capital-funding-plunges-globally-first-half-despite-ai-frenzy-2023-07-06/. Accessed 1 May 2024.

21  O'Brien, Amy, and Tim Smith. "SVB: Why Did so Many UK Startups Only Have One Bank Account?" *Sifted*, 16 Mar. 2023, https://sifted.eu/articles/svb-uk-startups-one-bank-account. Accessed 1 May 2024.

22  "Explainer: What Caused Silicon Valley Bank's Failure?" *Reuters*, 10 Mar. 2023, https://www.reuters.com/business/finance/what-caused-silicon-valley-banks-failure-2023-03-10/. Accessed 1 May 2024.

23  Hammond, George. "US Venture Capital Fundraising Hits a 6-Year Low." *Financial Times*, 5 Jan. 2024, https://www.ft.com/content/cfb186c8-22f4-4a82-b262-f4380a5d82b8. Accessed 1 May 2024.

24  Quinn, William, and John D. Turner. *Boom and Bust*. Cambridge University Press, 2020, p. 7.

25  See, for example:
Quinn, William, and John D. Turner. *Boom and Bust*. Cambridge University Press, 2020, p. 193.
And:
Callahan, Gene, and Roger Garrison. "Does Austrian Business Cycle Theory Help Explain the Dot-Com Boom and Bust?" *The Quarterly Journal of Austrian Economics*, vol. 6, no. 2, July 2003, https://cdn.mises.org/qjae6_2_3.pdf. Accessed 1 May 2024.

26  Quinn, William, and John D. Turner. *Boom and Bust*. Cambridge University Press, 2020, p. 193.

27  Quinn, William, and John D. Turner. *Boom and Bust*. Cambridge University Press, 2020, p. 193.

28  Murphy, Robert P. "My Reply to Krugman on Austrian Business-Cycle Theory." *Mises.org*, 24 Jan. 2011, https://mises.org/library/my-reply-krugman-austrian-business-cycle-theory. Accessed 1 May 2024.

29  "NRC - Historical Time Series." *US Census Bureau*, https://www.census.gov/construction/nrc/data/series.html. Accessed 1 May 2024.

30  Quinn, William, and John D. Turner. *Boom and Bust*. Cambridge University Press, 2020, p. 208.

31  Woodford, Michael. "Convergence in Macroeconomics: Elements of the New Synthesis." *American Economic Journal: Macroeconomics*, vol. 1, no. 1, Jan. 2009, pp. 267–79, https://doi.org/10.1257/mac.1.1.267.

32  Garrison, Roger W. *Time and Money*. Routledge, 2002.

33  Hazlitt, Henry. *Economics in One Lesson: The Shortest & Surest Way to Understand Basic Economics*. Crown, 2014 (reprint edition), pp. 186–187 (chapter 14, section 3).

34  Bharathan, Vipin. "The 'Minsky Moment' Drags On: The Financial Instability Hypothesis and Its Lessons." *Forbes*, 6 July 2023, https://www.forbes.com/sites/vipinbharathan/2023/07/

06/the-minsky-moment-drags-on-the-financial-instability-hypothesis-and-its-lessons/. Accessed 1 May 2024.

35  Whalen, Charles J. *The US Credit Crunch of 2007: A Minsky Moment*. 2007, https://www.econstor.eu/bitstream/10419/54321/1/557644089.pdf. Accessed 1 May 2024.

36  Lucas, Robert E. "Econometric Policy Evaluation: A Critique." *Carnegie-Rochester Conference Series on Public Policy*, vol. 1, Jan. 1976, pp. 19–46, https://doi.org/10.1016/s0167-2231(76)80003-6.

37  "What's a Bubble? (Podcast Transcript)." *Planet Money*, 1 Nov. 2013, https://www.npr.org/sections/money/2013/11/01/242351065/episode-493-whats-a-bubble-nobel-edition. Accessed 1 May 2024.

38  Garrison, Roger W. *Time and Money*. Routledge, 2002. See "Meeting the challenge to the Austrian theory" (Chapter 2).

39  Snowdon, Brian, and Howard R. Vane. *Modern Macroeconomics: Its Origins, Development and Current State*. Edward Elgar, 2014. See chapter by Paul Davidson.

40  "It Is Difficult to Get a Man to Understand Something When His Salary Depends upon His Not Understanding It." *Quote Investigator*, 30 Nov. 2017, https://quoteinvestigator.com/2017/11/30/salary/. Accessed 1 May 2024.

41  Minsky, Hyman. "The Financial Instability Hypothesis: A Restatement." *Hyman P. Minsky Archive*, Oct. 1978, https://digitalcommons.bard.edu/hm_archive/180/. Accessed 1 May 2024.

42  See, for example:
Murphy, Robert P. "My Reply to Krugman on Austrian Business-Cycle Theory." *Mises.org*, 24 Jan. 2011, https://mises.org/library/my-reply-krugman-austrian-business-cycle-theory. Accessed 1 May 2024.
And:
Murphy, Robert P. "Rebutting Paul Krugman on the 'Austrian' Pandemic." *The Independent Institute*, 8 Sept. 2021, https://www.independent.org/news/article.asp?id=13751. Accessed 1 May 2024.

43  Charles, Sébastien. "Is Minsky's Financial Instability Hypothesis Valid?" *Cambridge Journal of Economics*, vol. 40, no. 2, 2016, pp. 427–36, https://www.jstor.org/stable/24695915.

44 Krugman, Paul. "The Hangover Theory." *Slate*, 4 Dec. 1998, https://slate.com/business/1998/12/the-hangover-theory.html. Accessed 1 May 2024.

45 Keen, Steve. *The New Economics*. John Wiley & Sons, 2021, p. 125.

46 Keen, Steve. *The New Economics*. John Wiley & Sons, 2021, p. 66.

47 Keen, Steve. *The New Economics*. John Wiley & Sons, 2021, p. 135..

48 Mcleay, Michael, et al. "Money Creation in the Modern Economy." *Bank of England Quarterly Bulletin 2014 Q1*, 14 Mar. 2014, https://www.bankofengland.co.uk/-/media/boe/files/quarterly-bulletin/2014/money-creation-in-the-modern-economy. Accessed 1 May 2024.

49 Mcdonald, John F. *Rethinking Macroeconomics a History of Economic Thought Perspective*. London Routledge, 2022, p. 29.

50 Wigglesworth, Robin. "ZIRP: Good, Actually!" *Financial Times*, 19 Sept. 2023, https://www.ft.com/content/77b98af7-4089-4d1e-9eb1-e42053813aa2. Accessed 1 May 2024.

51 Cunningham, Paul, et al. "The Impact of Direct Support to R&D and Innovation in Firms." *Nesta*, Jan. 2013, https://media.nesta.org.uk/documents/the_impact_of_direct_support_to_rd_and_innovation_in_firms.pdf. Accessed 1 May 2024.

52 Cunningham, Paul, et al. "The Impact of Direct Support to R&D and Innovation in Firms." *Nesta*, Jan. 2013, https://media.nesta.org.uk/documents/the_impact_of_direct_support_to_rd_and_innovation_in_firms.pdf. Accessed 1 May 2024. P. 29.

53 "[Withdrawn] Smart Funding: Assessment of Impact and Evaluation of Processes." *GOV.UK*, 13 Oct. 2015, https://www.gov.uk/government/publications/smart-funding-assessment-of-impact-and-evaluation-of-processes. Accessed 1 May 2024.

54 Archived report available at: https://web.archive.org/web/20190725114541/https://assets.publishing.service.gov.uk/government/uploads/system/uploads/attachment_data/file/467204/Smart_Evaluation_-_Final_Final_Report_7_October.pdf

55 Cunningham, Paul, et al. "The Impact of Direct Support to R&D and Innovation in Firms." *Nesta*, Jan. 2013, https://media.nesta.

org.uk/documents/the_impact_of_direct_support_to_rd_and_innovation_in_firms.pdf. Accessed 1 May 2024.

56  Arnold, Erik, and Martin Wörter. "Evaluation of the Austrian Industrial Research Promotion Fund (FFF) and the Austrian Science Fund (FWF) Synthesis Report Report." *ETH Zürich*, 2004, https://doi.org/10.3929/ethz-a-004755768. Accessed 1 May 2024. P. 53.

57  Hazlitt, Henry. *Economics in One Lesson: The Shortest & Surest Way to Understand Basic Economics*. Crown, 2014 (reprint edition). P. 45.

## CHAPTER 5: RECIPES FOR UNPRODUCTIVITY

1  Pringle, Eleanor. "Google Overhired Talent to Do 'Fake Work' and Stop Them Working for Rivals, Claims Former PayPal Boss Keith Rabois." *Fortune*, 10 Mar. 2023, https://fortune.com/2023/03/10/google-over-hired-talent-do-nothing-fake-work-stop-working-rivals-former-paypal-boss-keith-rabois/. Accessed 1 May 2024.

2  Kay, Grace. "A Laid-off Meta Worker Says the Company Paid Her to Not Work: They Were 'Hoarding Us like Pokémon Cards.'" *Business Insider*, 14 Mar. 2023, https://www.businessinsider.com/laid-off-meta-employee-says-paid-not-to-work-2023-3. Accessed 1 May 2024.

3  Kay, Hugh Langley, Grace. "Inside the Perverse System of 'Lazy Management' That's Destroying the Tech Industry." *Business Insider*, 10 July 2023, https://www.businessinsider.com/tech-industry-fake-work-problem-bad-managers-bosses-layoffs-jobs-2023-7. Accessed 1 May 2024.

4  Thier, Jane. "The Double Life of a Gen Z Google Software Engineer Earning Six Figures Who Says He Works 1 Hour a Day." *Fortune*, 20 Aug. 2023, https://fortune.com/2023/08/20/gen-z-google-one-hour-workday-2/. Accessed 1 May 2024.

5  Chen, Te-Ping. "These Tech Workers Say They Were Hired to Do Nothing." *Wall Street Journal*, 7 Apr. 2023, https://www.wsj.com/amp/articles/these-tech-workers-say-they-were-hired-to-do-nothing-762ff158. Accessed 1 May 2024.

6   Pringle, Eleanor. "Google Overhired Talent to Do 'Fake Work' and Stop Them Working for Rivals, Claims Former PayPal Boss Keith Rabois." *Fortune*, 10 Mar. 2023, https://fortune.com/2023/03/10/google-over-hired-talent-do-nothing-fake-work-stop-working-rivals-former-paypal-boss-keith-rabois/. Accessed 1 May 2024.

7   Highsmith, Jim. "History: The Agile Manifesto," 2001, https://agilemanifesto.org/history.html. Accessed 1 May 2024.

8   "Principles behind the Agile Manifesto," 2001, https://agilemanifesto.org/principles.html. Accessed 1 May 2024.

9   Parkinson, Cyril Northcote. "Parkinson's Law." *The Economist*, 19 Nov. 1955, https://www.economist.com/news/1955/11/19/parkinsons-law. Accessed 1 May 2024.

10  Brooks, Frederick. *The Mythical Man-Month*. Addison-Wesley, 1995.

11  Cagle, Kurt. "The End of Agile." *Forbes*, 23 Aug. 2019, https://www.forbes.com/sites/cognitiveworld/2019/08/23/the-end-of-agile/. Accessed 1 May 2024.

12  Ries, Eric. *The Lean Startup: How Constant Innovation to Creates Radically Successful Businesses*. Portfolio Penguin, 2011. See introduction.

13  Ries, Eric. "Venture Hacks Interview: 'What Is the Minimum Viable Product?'" *Startup Lessons Learned*, 29 Mar. 2009, https://www.startuplessonslearned.com/2009/03/minimum-viable-product.html. Accessed 1 May 2024.

14  Blank, Steve. "Why the Lean Start-up Changes Everything." *Harvard Business Review*, May 2013, https://hbr.org/2013/05/why-the-lean-start-up-changes-everything. Accessed 1 May 2024.

15  Blodget, Henry. "Mark Zuckerberg on Innovation." *Business Insider*, Oct. 2009, https://www.businessinsider.com/mark-zuckerberg-innovation-2009-10. Accessed 1 May 2024.

16  Ulwick, Tony. https://www.linkedin.com/posts/tonyulwick_which-approach-to-product-innovation-makes-activity-7076901874058047489-W8uW/. Accessed 1 May 2024.

17  See:
    Dowd, Kevin. "Meet Mark Zuckerberg's Harvard Classmate

Who Is Trying to Build a Global Startup Factory." *Forbes*, 4 May 2022, https://www.forbes.com/sites/kevindowd/2022/05/04/meet-mark-zuckerbergs-harvard-classmate-who-is-trying-to-build-a-global-startup-factory/. Accessed 1 May 2024.
And:
Lewin, Amy. "Entrepreneurs on Acid." *Sifted*, 20 Feb. 2019, https://sifted.eu/articles/entrepreneur-first-struggles-at-scale. Accessed 1 May 2024.

18  See:
"1,000+ Investments from Day Zero." *Antler*, 19 Dec. 2023, https://www.antler.co/blog/1000-investments-from-day-zero. Accessed 1 May 2024.
And:
Nicol-Schwarz, Kai. "In Data: The Entrepreneur First Portfolio." *Sifted*, 16 Sept. 2021, https://sifted.eu/articles/entrepreneur-first-portfolio. Accessed 1 May 2024.

19  Lewin, Amy. "Entrepreneurs on Acid." *Sifted*, 20 Feb. 2019, https://sifted.eu/articles/entrepreneur-first-struggles-at-scale. Accessed 1 May 2024.

20  Kay, Grace. "A Laid-off Meta Worker Says the Company Paid Her to Not Work: They Were 'Hoarding Us like Pokémon Cards.'" *Business Insider*, 14 Mar. 2023, https://www.businessinsider.com/laid-off-meta-employee-says-paid-not-to-work-2023-3. Accessed 1 May 2024.

21  Orlowski, Andrew. "How Idleness at Work Became an Epidemic That Is Wrecking Britain." *The Telegraph*, 7 Apr. 2023, https://www.telegraph.co.uk/technology/2023/04/07/how-idleness-at-work-became-an-epidemic-wrecking-britain/. Accessed 1 May 2024.

## CHAPTER 6: WHAT WE CAN DO

1  Wasserman, Noam. "The Founder's Dilemma." *Harvard Business Review*, Feb. 2008, https://hbr.org/2008/02/the-founders-dilemma. Accessed 1 May 2024.

2  Head, Greg. "Mailchimp Is a Bootstrap Unicorn. Why so Little Media Coverage?" *Practical Founders*, 29 Oct. 2021, https://practicalfounders.com/articles/mailchimp-bootstrap-unicorn-little-media-coverage/. Accessed 1 May 2024.

3   "Safer - a Better Way to Fund Startups." *Next Wave*, https://nextwave.partners/safer. Accessed 1 May 2024.

4   Mulcahy, Diane, et al. *We Have Met the Enemy…and He Is Us: Lessons from Twenty Years of the Kauffman Foundation's Investments in Venture Capital Funds and the Triumph of Hope over Experience.* May 2012, p. 34, https://doi.org/10.2139/ssrn.2053258.

5   Palihapitiya, Chamath. "2018 Annual Letter." *Social Capital*, 2018, https://www.socialcapital.com/ideas/2018-annual-letter. Accessed 30 Apr. 2024.

6   John Maynard Keynes. *The General Theory of Employment, Interest and Money; the Economic Consequences of the Peace.* Wordsworth Editions, 2017, p. 112.

7   John Maynard Keynes. *The General Theory of Employment, Interest and Money; the Economic Consequences of the Peace.* Wordsworth Editions, 2017, p. 112–113.

8   John Maynard Keynes. *The General Theory of Employment, Interest and Money; the Economic Consequences of the Peace.* Wordsworth Editions, 2017, p. 278.

9   Gyori, Benjamin Jozef, et al. "Shelf with Integrated Electronics." *US Patent*, 19 June 2015, https://patents.google.com/patent/US10064502B1. Accessed 1 May 2024.

10  Cohn, Jonathan Evan. "Ultrasonic Bracelet and Receiver for Detecting Position in 2d Plane." *US Patent*, 28 Mar. 2016, https://patents.google.com/patent/US20170278051. Accessed 1 May 2024.

11  "Introducing Amazon Go and the World's Most Advanced Shopping Technology." *Amazon*, YouTube Video, 5 Dec. 2016, https://www.youtube.com/watch?v=NrmMk1Myrxc. Accessed 1 May 2024.

12  Natt Garun. "Amazon Just Launched a Cashier-Free Convenience Store." *The Verge*, The Verge, 5 Dec. 2016, https://www.theverge.com/2016/12/5/13842592/amazon-go-new-cashier-less-convenience-store. Accessed 1 May 2024.

13  Kastrenakes, Jacob. "Amazon's Cashier-Free Store Reportedly Breaks If More than 20 People Are in It." *The Verge*, 27 Mar. 2017, https://www.theverge.com/2017/3/27/15073468/amazon-go-shopper-tracking-store-opening-delay. Accessed 1 May 2024.

14　Soper, Spencer. "Bloomberg - Are You a Robot?" *Bloomberg*, 19 Sept. 2018, https://www.bloomberg.com/news/articles/2018-09-19/amazon-is-said-to-plan-up-to-3-000-cashierless-stores-by-2021. Accessed 1 May 2024.

15　Grant, Katie. "Amazon Fresh's Futuristic Cashierless Stores Fail to Compete with Tesco and Aldi." *inews*, 26 Jan. 2023, https://inews.co.uk/news/consumer/amazon-fresh-stores-fail-compete-tesco-aldi-2108847. Accessed 1 May 2024.

16　Singh, Rimjhim. "Amazon's 'Just Walk Out' Checkout Tech Was Powered by 1,000 Indian Workers." *Business Standard*, 4 Apr. 2024, https://www.business-standard.com/companies/news/amazon-s-just-walk-out-checkout-tech-was-powered-by-1-000-indian-workers-124040400463_1.html. Accessed 1 May 2024.

17　"Amazon's 'Just Walk Out' Pivot: Reimagining Tech." *PYMNTS*, 8 Apr. 2024, https://www.pymnts.com/amazon/2024/amazons-just-walk-out-pivot-reimagining-tech/. Accessed 1 May 2024.

18　Palmer, Annie. "Amazon Ditches Cashierless Checkout System at Its Grocery Stores." *CNBC*, 3 Apr. 2024, https://www.cnbc.com/2024/04/03/amazon-ditches-cashierless-checkout-system-at-its-grocery-stores.html. Accessed 1 May 2024.

19　Kniberg, Henrik, and Anders Ivarsson. "Scaling Agile @ Spotify with Tribes, Squads, Chapters & Guilds." *Crisp's Blog*, Oct. 2012, https://blog.crisp.se/wp-content/uploads/2012/11/SpotifyScaling.pdf. Accessed 1 May 2024.

20　Ulrickk, Tony. https://www.linkedin.com/posts/tonyulwick_when-companies-get-innovation-wrong-its-activity-7066382368256733185-BF61. Accessed 1 May 2024.

## FINAL THOUGHTS

1　Denker, John S. *See How It Flies*. https://www.av8n.com/how/. Accessed 1 May 2024.

# INDEX

2.5x return. *See* venture capital
4chan.org   59
10x Illusion, the. *See* start-ups; moat illusions
10x product
   *description of*   58
Agile   140–148, 159, 179
   (2001) *Software Development Manifesto*   140–142
   (2019) *as a religion, Forbes article*   149
Agoda   55
AI. *See* artificial intelligence
Airbnb   14, 108, 153, 164
air taxis. *See* eVTOLs
Alibaba   108
Amazon   8, 46, 64, 67, 135, 175–176
   (2015) *smart shelf patent*   176
   (2016) *Just Walk Out*   176
   (2016) *ultrasonic signal patent*   176
   (2023) *layoffs*   16
   *staff bloating*   135–136
Amazon Go   176–178
Andreessen Horowitz   81, 82, 85, 92, 93
   (2021) *funds raised*   81
   (2022) *accusation of staking fees*   82
angel investors   171
Apple   62, 67, 94, 167

Archer   28
   *investment in*   29
artificial intelligence   18, 26, 94, 138, 150–151, 151, 162, 164, 176
   *open-source AI*   58
augmented reality   138, 164
Austrian school theory. *See* business cycle
autonomous cars. *See* self-driving cars
aviation sector   162
banking sector
   *start-up challenges*   19–23
Bankman-Fried, Sam   90–91
Bank of England   101, 103, 104, 105, 107
   (2014) *article debunking effect of new money*   120
Benchmark   51
BenevolentAI   26–28, 30
   (2012) *shares*   27
   (2015) *investment*   26
   (2018) *investment*   26
   (2019) *investment*   26
   *BEN-2293*   27
Blank, Steve   152
blockchain   18, 93, 138, 162, 164
Bloomberg   109, 176
Bogan, Vicki   89
Booking.com   49–50, 52, 54
   *companies owned*   55

bootstrapping 169
Brand Illusion, the. *See* start-ups; moat illusions; brand illusion, the
Brooks, Fred 146
business cycle 113, 114
  *Austrian school theory 114–120*
  *financial instability hypothesis 115*
  *post-Keynesian school theory 114–120*
Business Insider 135
Cambridge Associates 76
Canva 64
Charles Tyrwhitt 19
chase yield 100
ChatGPT 57–59, 94. *See also* OpenAI
Chowdhury, Hasan 26
CNBC 109
Coinbase
  *(2023) layoffs 16*
copycats. *See* start-ups; copycats
Coursera 133
COVID-19 pandemic 104, 105, 106, 109
cryptocurrency 9, 68, 90, 119
Deliveroo 45
Dell
  *(2023) layoffs 16*
Disney 32
DocuSign 45
dot-com bubble 9, 13, 26, 77, 90, 111, 121
  *(2000) bursting of 112*
Dott
  *(2023) shuts down in London 48*

*investments in* 47
DreamWorks 32
Dropbox
  *(2023) layoffs 16*
eBay 32
e-bike 47–48
economies of scale 60
ESG bubble 120–121
European Central Bank 101, 103
  *negative interest rate 104*
European Investment Fund 77
European Union 123, 124
Eventbrite 45
evergreen funds 172
eVTOLs 28–31
  *main impediment to development 28*
  *Midnight 28*
Expedia 49, 55
  *affiliate partnership with Hopper 56*
  *companies owned 55*
Exxon 121
Facebook 64, 67, 71, 108, 146
Fama, Eugene 116
Fed. *See* U.S. Federal Reserve
Federal Aviation Administration 29
federal funds rate 101, 104, 107
  *(2022) rate of increase 107*
Feld, Brad 81
Fibonacci sequence 142, 144
financial crisis, the (2008) 99, 103, 115, 174
financial instability hypothesis 115

| | |
|---|---|
| Financial Times | 95, 108, 120 |
| Fiverr | 45 |
| Flow | 92 |
|    *investment raised* | *92* |
| flying cars. *See* eVTOLs | |
| Forbes | 67, 75, 149 |
| Fortune | 82, 135, 136 |
| FTX | 9, 39, 41, 68, 95 |
|    *(2019) launch* | *90* |
|    *(2021) investments raised* | *90* |
|    *investment in* | *38* |
| Future Fund | 35 |
| generative AI | 93 |
| GitHub | |
|    *(2023) layoffs* | *16* |
| Global Founders Capital | 21 |
| Goldman Sachs | 51 |
| Goodwin, Tom | 108 |
| Google | 8, 62–64, 67, 135–136, 138 |
|    *(2023) default smartphone search engine* | *62* |
|    *(2023) leaked chatbot memo* | *58* |
|    *DeepMind* | *37* |
|    *invents core technology behind ChatGPT* | *58* |
|    *staff bloating* | *135* |
| Google Ventures | 24 |
| government bonds | 102 |
| government grants. *See* start-ups;government grants | |
| Graham, Paul | 17, 25 |
|    *description of a start-up* | *17* |
| Greater Fool Theory | 88–90, 94 |
| Great Moderation, the | 111 |
| greedflation 107. *See also* inflation | |
| green technology | 121 |

| | |
|---|---|
| Greenwald, Bruce | 57, 61, 63 |
| Harvard Management Company | 51 |
| Harvard University | 51 |
| Hayek, Friedrich | 114 |
| Hazlitt, Henry | 126 |
| Helmers, Hamilton | 63 |
| Hern, Alex | 108 |
| Hinduja, Karam | 78, 89, 90, 93 |
| Hopper | 54–56 |
|    *(2014) launch* | *54* |
|    *(2017) adding hotel booking* | *55* |
|    *(2023) layoffs* | *56* |
|    *(2023) trouble with Expedia* | *56* |
|    *investments raised* | *54, 55* |
| Horizon 2020 | 123 |
| Horizon Europe | 124 |
| Hotels.com | 55 |
| Hotwire.com | 55 |
| Housenbold, Jeffrey | 48 |
| housing market | |
|    *(2008) crash* | *112* |
|    *boom* | *112* |
|    *bubble* | *112* |
| HSBC | 102, 105 |
|    *(2022) acquires SVB* | *110* |
| HumanForest | |
|    *investments in* | *47* |
| Indeed | |
|    *(2023) layoffs* | *16* |
| inflation | 106 |
|    *(2021) global* | *107* |
| Instagram | 36, 71 |
| interest rate | 99–111, 114 |
|    *(2000) dotcom bubble bursting* | *112* |
|    *(2001) lowering of* | *112* |
|    *(2002) lowering of* | *112* |

(2021) fueling VC activity  109
(2022) investments into startups collapse  109
(2023) six-year low in investment  109
International Monetary Fund (IMF)  105
internet
  (2000) amount raised by VCs for start-ups  81
  late 1990s  13, 111
investment in tech sector. *See also* venture capitalists
  (2022) decline of  16
  (2023) decline of  16
  facilitating innovation  25
investment management company. *See* venture capital firm
iPhones  50
IPO. *See* start-ups;initial public offering
IRR. *See* venture capital fund; internal rate of return
Johansson, Eric  30
JPMorgan Chase  51
Juicero  9, 23, 94, 101, 121, 127, 153, 175
  (2016) launch  24
  (2017) going bust  25
  (2017) layoffs  24
Kauffman Foundation  83, 87, 96, 97
  (2012) analyze 20 years of investing in VC funds  83
Kayak  55
Keen, Steve  119
Keynes, John Maynard  115, 173
King, Mervyn  107

Kleiner Perkins  23
Krugman, Paul  118
lean start-up methodology  151
Lewin, Amy  157
Lime  48
  investments in  47
limited partners 69, 70, 73, 76, 85, 109, 172
  2.5x return  73
  misalignment with VCs  82
LinkedIn  52, 65, 167
Litvak, Katherine  83
Long-Term Capital Management
  (1998) collapse of  111
Loot
  (2014) development of  19
  (2016) investment  21
  (2018) investment  22
  (2019) going bust  22
  (2019) investment  22
  funding difficulties  20–22
Lowe, Derek  27
LPs. *See* limited partners
Lucas. Robert  116
Lyft  45
Mailchimp  167, 169
  company sold  167
malinvestment  114
Masters, Brooke  39
Mercedes Benz  63
Meta  37, 58, 135, 138, 146, 158
  (2023) layoffs  16
  leak on 4chan.org  59
  staff bloating  135
metaverse  18
meta-work  146–147

Microsoft 67
  *(2023) layoffs*   *16*
Mills, D. Quinn 26
minimum viable product 152–157
Minsky, Hyman 115, 118
Minsky moment. *See* financial crisis, the (2008)
Mistral 36–38, 155
  *investment in*   *37*
moat illusions. *See* start-ups; moat illusions
moats. *See* start-ups; moats
Molla, Rani 45
Momondo 55
Munger, Charlie 67, 81
Murphy, Robert D. 112
Murthy, Narayana 89
MVP. *See* minimum viable product
NASDAQ 14
natural monopoly 62
Nespresso 23
Netflix 18, 32, 36, 60, 153
  *(2022) The Crown, cost of*   *60*
network effect 108.
  *See* start-ups; moats
Neumann, Adam 88, 90, 91, 93
  *(2019) cashes out WeWork shares privately*   *88*
New Synthesis 113
NewTV. *See* Quibi
New York Stock Exchange 45, 71
NFTs 93
O'Mara, Margaret 38, 91
Ontario Teachers' Pension Plan 41

OpenAI 37, 57–59
  *(2022) ChatGPT launch*   *57*
  *(2022) investments raised*   *58*
  *(2023) leaked Google memo*   *58*
  *(2024) launch marketplace*   *59*
opportunity cost 175
Orbitz 55
Palantir 45
Paramount Pictures 33
Paris Air Show 28
Parkinson, Cyril Northcote 145
Parkinson's Law 145
patents. *See* start-ups
PayPal
  *(2023) layoffs*   *16*
Peloton
  *marketing campaigns*   *44*
Phalippou, Ludovic 88
pharmaceutical industry 26
Pinterest 45
pitch decks 69. *See also* start-ups; pitch decks
pivot 152
Planning Poker 142
Ponzi schemes 11, 83–88
post-Keynesian school theory. *See* business cycle
Power Corporation 22
Priceline 49, 55
Prime 36
QE. *See* quantitative easing
quantitative easing 101–106, 112, 116
  *central bank assets*   *104*
Quibi 9, 32–37, 44, 61, 153, 175
  *(2018) launch*   *32*

*advertising campaigns*　　34
　　*Forbes article*　　33
　　*investment raised*　　33
　　*shuts down*　　35
Quinn, William　　111, 120
rationality　　116, 118
R & D　　120, 124
Reddit　　45
Ries, Eric　　151
Robinhood　　45
Robotics　　94
Rocket Science Group　　167
Royal Bank of Scotland　　22, 40
SaaS (software as a service)　　18
Salesforce
　　*(2023) layoffs*　　16
Samsung　　62
Scale Illusion, the. *See* start-ups; moat illusions; scale illusion, the
Scott, Fredrick D.　　78
Scrum　　141, 142, 143, 146, 147
Scrum Master　　148
SEC　　122
Seed Enterprise Investment Scheme　　127–128
SEIS. *See* Seed Enterprise Investment Scheme
self-driving cars　　31, 93
Sequoia Capital　　76, 81, 90
　　*(2018-2022) funds raised*　　81
Silicon Valley　　15, 24, 28, 94
　　*(2000s) layoffs of*　　14
Silicon Valley Bank　　109, 110
　　*(2022) bank run and collapse*　　110

Sinclair, Upton　　117
Snapchat　　45
social networks　　14, 50
SoftBank　　51
Speedinvest　　21
Spotify　　18, 45, 179–180
　　*(2023) layoffs*　　16
　　*bottom line per year*　　44
sprint review　　143
sprints　　141
start-up factories　　155–157
start-ups 17–41, 43–65, 105–108, 114, 127–128, 151–153, 169
　　*(2010) venture capitalist investments*　　14
　　*(2020) venture capitalist investments*　　14
　　*(2021) venture capitalist investments*　　14
　　*Amazon archetype, the*　　45
　　*copycats*　　46–65
　　*description of*　　17
　　*desirable characteristics of founders*　　154–155
　　*founders*
　　　　*often kicked out*　　168
　　*government grants*　　122–129
　　　　*distortions*　　125–126
　　*importance of discovery*　　30–31
　　*initial public offering*　　71
　　*moat illusions*　　57–64
　　　　*10x Illusion, the*　　57–59
　　　　*Brand Illusion, the*　　62–64
　　　　*Scale Illusion, the*　　60–62
　　*moats*　　49–65
　　　　*Expedia & Booking.com*　　56
　　　　*network effect*　　50
　　　　*switching cost*　　50
　　*pattern of unprofitability by year*　　45–46

# INDEX

pitch decks 69
pre-seed & seed investments 36
runway 21
SaaS 18
start-up way, the 43, 55
story telling 90–94
technical uncertainty 30
valuation 69

SVB. *See* Silicon Valley Bank

switching cost. *See* start-ups; moats

tech sector 131–159, 161–182, 174
  (2021) extravaganza 14–16, 15
  (2022) layoffs 133
  bloating and over staffing 131–159
  task bloating 140–145

Theranos 39, 68, 95, 122
  investment in 38

Thiel, Peter 58, 60, 75

Tier 48
  investments in 47

Tiffany's 63

TikTok 32, 34

Travelocity 55

Twilio 45
  (2023) layoffs 16

Twitter 7–8, 134
  (2023) layoffs 16, 134

Uber 14, 18, 31–32, 45, 108, 164

Uber Black 28

unicorn boom 107–110, 127

unicorn bubble 101, 113

unicorn status 14

U.S. checking accounts, total balances of 106

U.S. Federal Reserve 101–103, 104, 105, 111
  (1998) interest rate lowered 111
  (2000) response to dotcom bubble bursting 112
  (2008-2010) assets purchased 103

U.S. Government Bonds 100

U.S. National Bureau of Economic Research (NBER) 76

U.S. Securities and Exchange Commission 53

valuation 69. *See also* start-ups

VC. *See* venture capital

venture capital 67–97, 105, 120, 124. *See also* venture capitalists
  2.5x return 77
  carry 70
  exit 70
  (2021-2023) money generated 110
  firm 68, 105, 109, 154–155
  management fees 80–83, 172
  funds 15, 68, 117, 128, 168, 171–172
  (1984-2018) average return by launch year 76
  (2012) returns reported by VCs over time 84
  (2016) study on fund managers manipulating reports 85
  (2020) Cambridge Associates report 76
  internal rate of return 87–89
  methodologies of calculating unrealized gains 85–87
  results, the 76–80
  power law 73–76
  rule of thirds 73–76, 77
  SAFE 171
  SAFER 171
  secondary sale 72

venture capitalists  22–23, 59, 65, 114, 171
   *(2010) start-up investments*  *14*
   *(2016) unicorn survey*  *15*
   *(2020) start-up investments*  *14*
   *(2021) start-up investments*  *14*
   *due diligence, lack of*  *34–41*
Vertical Aerospace  28
vertiport  29
video streaming  32–37
Vimeo
   *(2023) layoffs*  *16*
von Mises, Ludwig  114
Vroom  45
Wall Street  89
Wall Street Journal  109
Washington Post  8
Wasserman, Noam  169
waterfall methodology  140
Wayfair  45
Waymo
   *(2023) layoffs*  *16*
WD-40  64
Western Economic Association Conference  119
WeWork 9, 43–44, 51–54, 63–64, 75, 88, 90–91, 101
   *(2019) CEO resignation*  *53*
   *(2023) filing for bankruptcy*  *54*
   *investments raised*  *51*
X. *See* Twitter
Yahoo
   *(2023) layoffs*  *16*
YouTube  36
zero interest rate policy  99–101, 108–109, 111–112, 116
Zillow  45
ZIRP. *See* zero interest rate policy
Zoom  91
   *(2023) layoffs*  *16*
Zuckerberg, Mark  152

ALSO BY THE AUTHOR:

Emmanuel Maggiori, PhD

# SMART UNTIL IT'S DUMB

Why artificial intelligence keeps making epic mistakes (and why the AI bubble will burst)